THE CPD CO-ORDINATOR'S TOOLKIT

THE CPD CO-ORDINATOR'S TOOLKIT

Sue Kelly

PCP
Paul Chapman
Publishing

Paul Chapman Publishing
A SAGE Publications Company
1 Oliver's Yard
55 City Road
London EC1Y 1SP

SAGE Publications Inc
2455 Teller Road
Thousand Oaks, California 91320

SAGE Publications India Pvt Ltd
B-42, Panchsheel Enclave
Post Box 4109
New Delhi 110 017

Library of Congress Control Number: 2006904386

A catalogue record for this book is available from the
British Library

ISBN-10 1-4129-2932-6   ISBN-13 978-1-4129-2932-5
ISBN-10 1-4129-2933-4   ISBN-13 978-1-4129-2933-2 (pbk)

Typeset by C&M Digitals (P) Ltd, Chennai, India
Printed in Great Britain by The Cromwell Press, Trowbridge Wiltshire
Printed on paper from sustainable resources

For you mum
Patricia Ann Kelly
8/12/1938–2/1/2006

CONTENTS

L IST OF FIGURES

*An asterisk denotes the figure which is on the CD only. All other figures can be found both in this book as a photocopiable and on the CD. These materials may be adapted to your own setting.

THE AUTHOR

Sue Kelly came back into mainstream teaching at the age of 33 following a period of nearly 10 years living in Madrid, where she had recruited and trained teachers for summer schools and taught English as a foreign language to business clients.

She was an English teacher at Millais School in Horsham, West Sussex before becoming an Assistant Headteacher, where she has responsibility for CPD amongst other things. Sue has taken part in the West Sussex County Council course for CPD co-ordinators and been a member of the TDA working party involved in the exemplification of the draft National Standards for teachers. Sue has completed the NCSL's NPQH programme, as part of her own ongoing CPD.

In addition to her school work, Sue can be found on Teachers' TV demonstrating the excellent approaches to CPD at her school. She also writes for magazines such as *CPD Update* and *Professional Development Today*, where her engaging style and practical approach offer valuable encouragement and ideas for those co-ordinators already in post or others considering taking on the role. Sue also writes the CPD section of the Open University's excellent website for teachers, www.TeachandLearn.net

Sue can be contacted at: skelly1@wsgfl.org.uk

ACKNOWLEDGEMENTS

I would like to say a huge thank you to everyone who has supported and helped me to put this book together, in particular the whole staff and the leadership group at Millais School, Horsham, West Sussex. Leon Nettley, my headteacher has played an instrumental part in developing the thinking behind some of the practical materials here, while I have included or been able to build on the work of Shirley Springer as staff development co-ordinator before me. As usual both teaching and support staff have helped to shape my ideas and been on the receiving end of implementing and trialling the different strategies to co-ordinate continuing professional development (CPD) practices. I can only say that seeing them on Teachers TV made me very proud of the professionalism and commitment which underpin this great school.

I am grateful to all the contributors to this book and hope the recognition of their good work is testament to it. I would especially like to thank Mel Wilde for reading my original article in *CPD Update* and without whom absolutely none of this would have been possible. Many other people, too numerous to mention, have given me invaluable encouragement along the way and, hopefully, they will know who they are, although thanks to Steve Davies who gave me the confidence I needed to continue with my work at exactly the time I needed it. Of course I must not forget Jude Bowen and the team at Paul Chapman Publishing for providing me with a great opportunity, and Charlotte Saunders for her helpful guidance.

I would like to thank my family and friends, without whose support I doubt this book would ever have been finished. Most of all I would like to thank my mum; I will always be indebted to her for the sacrifices she made and the love and encouragement she gave me unconditionally throughout my life.

PREFACE

This book has been written, and the various documents and pro formas put together, to support the practical day-to-day needs of those responsible for staff development in schools, colleges and other organizations where some of the same principles apply. I hope that it will go some way to supporting CPD co-ordinators to recognize and realize their own vision of CPD and save them time, energy and anxiety while doing so.

It is intended that the principles outlined in the book, and the practical materials through which to deliver them, extend to the broadest spectrum of individuals or groups. I am absolutely committed to the ongoing development of support staff in schools/colleges whose skills, knowledge, expertise and experiences outside our educational environment are often under-valued and under-used. With the recent workforce reform agenda it is more important than ever before that we consider how to meet the development needs of this key group of staff whose work is the foundation of successful educational institutions across the country.

I hope that CPD co-ordinators across all phases will recognize how many of these practical materials can be adapted (and improved!) for use in their particular context. While I have referred to heads of department or heads of faculty or team leaders, this of course does not exclude colleagues who are working in smaller schools in the primary or special schools phases who only have to consider how the practical tools can be adapted to suit them.

I am passionate about teaching and learning. I feel proud of the staff of my school for their active participation and ongoing commitment to their own development and the impact that this has on students in classrooms. Valuing the skills and knowledge of all staff in the school, deploying this effectively and engaging both staff and students in the processes of CPD means that we all play our part in the business of learning and make a real difference to pupils in classrooms. By involving everyone in your new approaches you will undoubtedly create a stimulating learning environment in your school – one in which every individual feels valued, motivated and inspired. I wish you luck!

Sue Kelly
April 2006

HOW TO USE THIS BOOK

The CD icon refers to material that is available on the CD which can be downloaded and adapted for your own use.

Understanding your role and where you are at present

This chapter will put you in a positive frame of mind to set about changing the culture of CPD practices in your school and give staff morale a boost at the same time. You can use the self-evaluation models as a quick and easy way to establish where you are in your school/institution in terms of CPD and begin to put together your own vision of where you would like to go. A selection of easily adaptable tools will get you off on the right foot along the road of best practice principles as set out by the Department for Education and Skills (DfES). Challenge the mindset of your staff to broaden their outlook on what constitutes effective CPD; boost confidence as colleagues realize just how much they have to offer as the new model of shared expertise takes hold and staff really value learning from each other. A series of ready-made PowerPoint slides will save you time as you articulate your vision clearly to the whole staff and can be effortlessly adapted to a variety of contexts. Support the practices of middle leaders/team leaders to gain extra momentum in managing and leading CPD for their own departments/teams by encouraging them to think through some key issues using the simple pro formas designed specifically for them.

Positive thinking

So – you are a CPD co-ordinator. Great! Welcome to what is perhaps the most exciting, if a little daunting, role in any school. Speaking from one co-ordinator to another, it is through our work and our vision of what constitutes creative and dynamic CPD practices that we can transform the learning culture in our schools. We can help to engage students more effectively so that they make even better progress in our classrooms and, at the same time, support staff to model life-long learning practices for pupils which will equip them with the skills and knowledge they need to lead happy, successful and fulfilled lives. What a privilege!

The need to model cost-effective approaches to CPD, rather than providing us with a constant headache, can become a driving force for those of us lucky enough to be given the role, as it forces us to think more imaginatively. The challenges we face in meeting and supporting the training and developmental needs of a diverse range of highly skilled support or teaching staff can become a catalyst for forcing us to think 'outside the box' and, by doing so, to take forward the practices in our schools to satisfying new places.

The overwhelming importance of our work to the stakeholders of the school or educational establishment where we are working is summed up succinctly by Roland Barthes: 'Probably nothing within a school has more impact on students in terms of skills' development, self confidence or classroom behaviour than the personal and professional development of their teachers' (Earley and Bubb, 2004: 17).

At a recent workshop I led for emerging CPD co-ordinators, I asked the delegates to sum up in one word how they felt about the huge responsibility of being in such a key role in their schools. The responses included such words as 'daunted', 'overwhelmed' and 'terrified'. Being in the position of CPD co-ordinator can make us feel all of those things but it can also make us feel excited, empowered and privileged, and that's why in my view it's the best job in the school.

So for those CPD co-ordinators who are still quite new to the role, those who may be interested in pursuing this as a next step in their career or who have been landed with the job, or for those who are dissatisfied with CPD practices in their school but have little idea of how to move them forward, or simply for experienced practitioners looking for some new ideas, the practical tools, advice and tips in this toolkit will provide something for everyone looking to build on current practices. The CPD co-ordinators I have spoken to who are anxious about their role in some way, have, without exception, found some comfort, motivation and a boost to their confidence in just knowing that they are not alone and that many of the experiences and challenges they face were exactly what I faced when I first began the job.

There are many interesting books on the subject of staff development written by people who, without doubt, understand the theory and the issues involved far better than I could ever hope to, but for those of us who are CPD co-ordinators out there doing the job there is little substitute for practical ideas and support from others in the same position. By sharing our ideas, as this book aims to do, we are already on the road to modelling effective CPD practices. It is as simple as that!

I have outlined in Figure 1.1 some of the challenges I faced initially when I took on the role of staff development co-ordinator in my school, many of which may be instantly recognizable to new or more experienced CPD co-ordinators. By judging your own school context against these simple indicators you can begin to gauge in practical and straightforward terms what areas of practice in your school may need some consideration to begin to shape your vision of where you wish CPD practices to go.

By spending a few minutes considering the challenges presented in Figure 1.1 and capturing your initial thoughts of how to begin to address them, you have the makings of your personal vision for CPD in your school/institution and the beginnings of a plan to effect some immediate, medium- and long-term changes. If you are not on the senior leadership team of your school, engage the support of someone who is and use the ideas or issues outlined above to open a dialogue for change; few things can be more important than this, given the potential impact on student learning and the improvement, if needed, on staff morale.

Figure 1.1 is a handy and easily referenced evaluation guide designed to get you thinking about CPD practices and how to tackle them. As a complement to it and as a more in-depth approach to considering current practices, I have found the self-evaluation table produced by London's

Learning Emerging, Developing, Establishing (EDE) project (see Figure 1.2 on the CD-ROM that accompanies this book) to be invaluable in moving forward areas of my practice in school.

There are obviously many ways of using such a model to support whole-school development practices. Although I have given some ideas here, your own school context will dictate how you might most successfully employ such a tool in identifying an area or areas which can form a part of your whole-school development plan to drive forward your vision successfully.

Figure 1.1 Informal self-evaluation of CPD leadership

Initial challenge/concern for author	This is the case in my school ✓ or ✗	Initial thoughts and ideas to move this forward
Perception of many staff that few opportunities for training were provided by me/the school		
Given the above, general disgruntlement and disaffection felt by some individuals regarding their own professional development		
General acceptance that external courses = professional development/training		
Lack of an adequate staff development budget to fund external courses = more disaffection and negative impact on staff morale		
Inability of CPD co-ordinator (in this case, me!) to conjure up significant sums of money to address the above		
Perception of the role of CPD co-ordinator among some staff as being one of control or having the power to deny or grant staff development opportunities		
Lack of any meaningful involvement or proactive engagement on the part of some staff in the process of their own ongoing professional development		
Reluctance of some staff to develop a professional portfolio		

Initial challenge/concern for author	This is the case in my school ✔ or ✗	Initial thoughts and ideas to move this forward
A generally ad hoc approach to the organization of development training at individual, departmental or whole school level. Little focused or meaningful matching of training/development activity(ies) to identified targets or objectives		
Lack of involvement of middle leaders/team leaders in supporting, leading or facilitating CPD practices for their subject/pastoral teams/those whom they line manage		
Classroom observations perceived by many/some staff as a perfunctory necessity to meet performance review requirements rather than as a developmental tool/opportunity for feedback for staff		
Little recognition or effective deployment of the skills and knowledge bank already in existence across the staff of the school		
Little real evaluation of the impact of staff development on students' learning and progress in the classroom		
Lack of a clear understanding of the school's position in relation to key principles of CPD practices or the tools to establish this		
Consequently, given the above, lack of vision for CPD in the school, i.e. where are we now and where do we want to be?		

P **Photocopiable: The CPD Co-ordinator's Toolkit**
Paul Chapman Publishing 2006 © Sue Kelly

An individual approach

Use your knowledge of staff development practices in your school to gauge your school's position across the areas of CPD and, drawing on Figure 1.2, establish whether these are 'emerging', 'developing' or 'establishing'. Record any evidence of CPD practices for each section and where this can be found if appropriate. Use this information to feed into a draft CPD action plan with clearly identified future objectives, realistic timescales and guaranteed success criteria. Include an idea of who will be involved and what their role(s) will be. Take this to your senior leadership team as a draft proposal and request their comments, feedback and support. Seek commitment to areas identified for change, that is, inclusion of key areas in the school improvement or development plan.

A consultative approach

Engage middle and senior leaders in reflecting on CPD practices in your school by sharing the self-evaluation with them and asking for feedback. Use the responses to set up some cross-curricular teams linked to senior leadership to consider and identify strengths and areas for development at this middle level. The sharing of expertise in CPD practices across these subjects/faculties will be part of this discussion and an added bonus. Use this working group to identify and prioritize areas for development. Engage them in the action planning process as above.

A networking approach

Take this opportunity to network with other schools and to learn from each other. Make the self-evaluation tool the focus for a specified number of network meetings of CPD co-ordinators in other schools either in your own locality or further afield. Working together with other colleagues will provide additional impetus to your work and open up an invaluable dialogue through which to exchange ideas and good practice.

Vivienne Porritt led the London's Learning project which created the Emerging, Developing, Establishing model. The framework is now available electronically and can be downloaded from www.lgfl.net/lgfl/sections/cpd/londonslearning/ede/.

Vivienne recommends using the EDE framework as an electronic tool and highlights two ideas for using the framework in this way:

✓ Paula Jones, Deputy Head of Chatsworth Infant School in Hounslow in London, uses the EDE framework electronically to traffic light aspects of the principles. This enables her to identify what is 'green for go' to spread practice across the school and what is amber and red as key elements to develop. This can be altered easily as practice changes and helps staff see development visually.

✓ In Waltham Forest, CPD leaders suggest using the framework to gather evidence for the statement and the choice of level. Using the framework electronically they insert 'Evidence is seen in …' and individuals and teams can then add evidence as support for Office for Standards in Education (Ofsted), Investors in People and school self-evaluation processes.

Points to remember

- Use self-evaluation tools to establish where your school is in terms of CPD practices.
- Use this evaluation process to establish key areas for development to be included on an action plan.
- Consult with and engage the support of your senior leadership team; key priorities for CPD should be included in your school improvement plan (SIP).
- Communicate your vision to others; articulate it clearly and confidently.

Making a start

When I first set out in my role as CPD co-ordinator I was immediately struck by the amount of power and control which staff suddenly perceived that I had. During the first few weeks in my new position I was constantly being asked to give permission for colleagues to attend a variety of external courses. Rather than feeling flattered with this new-found authority, I was completely perplexed for a variety of reasons:

- I realized that I didn't have a clue what I was doing.

- I didn't know how I could be expected to make decisions on what training was appropriate for each individual member of staff, given that there were 90 teaching staff and approximately 40 support staff in the school.

- I had a notion of cost-effectiveness, and simply saying yes to everyone who asked seemed at odds with it.

- The whole idea of the way staff were choosing a particular course to attend seemed to me a rather ad hoc process. When I asked if the course supported a particular personal or departmental target the answer was often vague.

- Staff seemed to be attending courses inconsistently across departments and, although much money was being spent, I detected that many staff were still very unhappy. This was often because some staff felt that it was always the same people attending external in-service training (Inset) and I was often informed, 'I haven't had any training for x number of years'. Whenever I asked what this meant, the reply was always the same: that the individual member of staff felt disgruntled because he or she had not been on a course during that time.

- Where did I start with what seemed to be an almost impossible task?

Many CPD co-ordinators, particularly in big primary or secondary schools, may well recognize this scenario from their own experience. Given that CPD has been very high on the government's agenda in recent years you may feel that the culture in your own school is far more forward thinking already in terms of what colleagues value as activities which constitute effective professional development. If not, or you wish to remind them, then you may find the pro forma in Figure 1.3 a useful tool in supporting staff to recognize that training opportunities and activities to help us develop our skills are happening all around us on a daily basis. One of the major challenges faced by CPD co-ordinators is the attitude of many staff who consider that going on courses is the only effective development training. By raising the awareness among staff of what constitutes effective ongoing development training we can have a very positive impact on staff morale.

One of the first things I did was to adapt the DfES list of 'Examples of CPD other than External Courses'. I enlarged the list of ideas in the light of my own school context, just as you can do for yours, and asked staff to tick off any activities in which they had been involved over the past 12 to 18 months and any activities which they felt would support their training needs in the immediate future. See the form in Figure 1.3.

This simple process had the following significant benefits:

✓ Staff began to recognize that a whole range of activities, many of which were already taking place on a daily basis, constitute effective developmental training.

✓ Attending an external course could now be seen as just one way to develop our skills, knowledge and understanding. (I sneakily put this last on the list!)

✓ Staff immediately began to feel better about the training opportunities they had been involved in as they were able to tick off a whole range of things in which they had taken part.

✓ Emphasis was placed not just on recognizing these activities but valuing the expertise of fellow colleagues and the idea that we can all learn from each other.

✓ Confidence was raised among staff as the potential for supporting each others' work, through effective deployment of the professional skills which each of us bring to our work, began to be realized.

✓ I now had an idea, albeit quite crude at this stage, of the kind of development activities which every member of the teaching staff felt would be appropriate for them to be involved in so as to develop professionally.

✓ This information could now be collated across department teams, line managers, pastoral and subject leaders, and could inform future planning for CPD; this had to be a positive step forward away from the ad hoc approaches of the past. This principle can be applied to any phase or size of school or other educational institution.

✓ All staff were actively engaged in the process of identifying potential development activities for themselves – a key element of good practice being the proactive engagement of individuals in the processes in place to develop them.

This simple pro forma provided the basis for moving forward the CPD practices in the school. In time it would be adapted to ensure that these activities were focused and targeted at identified needs rather than whims – but more of that later.

Points to remember

- Talk the talk – always use the term 'CPD activity' rather than 'course' for anything to do with developmental training and lead others on this.
- Recognize CPD as it happens in your school on a daily basis and talk it up.
- Support the work of others by encouraging creative and imaginative approaches to CPD.
- Use coaching models to disseminate good CPD practices across individuals and teams in your school.

Figure 1.3 Initial staff development pro forma

Member of staff: .... Department: .... Date: ....

Academic year 200X/200Y This year I have been involved in the following professional development activities:	Please tick	Evidence (Please select) When, where, what, with whom?	I would like to be involved in the following professional development activities next year (Please tick)
Observing good practitioners:			
Observing other teachers teaching			
Shadowing a colleague			
Visiting and seeing another school in action			
Observing and working with a visiting expert			
Extending professional experience:			
Leading and contributing to school-based Inset			
Rotation of roles/jobs			
Developing own professional profile			
Co-ordinating/managing a subject			
Assuming the role of leader for a special initiative in school			
Carrying out action research in the classroom/school			
Contributing to a professional publication			
Gaining experience of interviewing			
Acting as a performance reviewer			
Being reviewed			
Serving as a governor			
Serving on professional committee/working parties			
Becoming a union representative			

Academic year 200X/200Y This year I have been involved in the following professional development activities:	**Please tick**	**Evidence (Please select) When, where, what, with whom?**	**I would like to be involved in the following professional development activities next year (Please tick)**
Leading/supervising non-professionals who work in the classroom			
Working on extra-curricular activities			
Taking part in staff conferences on individual pupils			
Working with other professionals such as education psychologists			
Working with an exam board or marking exam papers			
Networking and sharing with a group of colleagues from another school			
Team teaching			
Learning through professional practice with others			
Developing pedagogy in the context of ICT			
Peer mentoring, e.g. mentoring a NQT			
Organizing a display in collaboration with colleagues			
Working with pupils:			
Taking responsibility for a group of pupils on an off-site visit			
Developing teaching skills across a wide age and ability range			
Working with pupils on school councils			
Working with pupils to present an assembly, play, musical performance or other event			

Academic year 200X/200Y This year I have been involved in the following professional development activities:	Please tick	Evidence (Please select) When, where, what, with whom?	I would like to be involved in the following professional development activities next year (Please tick)
Working with pupils preparing a school year book			
Collaborating with peripatetic teachers			
Mentoring individual pupils			
Taking time to evaluate your own practice: Inviting your peers to observe you			
Getting feedback from your own pupils			
Analyzing class and examination work			
Integrating the use of pupil websites and online communities into teaching			
Using e-mail/videoconferencing between pupils in teaching			
Negotiating targets and evaluating work alongside pupils			
Reviewing your marking			
Videoing yourself			
Other: In-house training: at departmental/whole-school level			
ICT training in-house			
International exchange or visit			
Aspiring Leader Conference			
External/county courses			

A copy of this completed pro forma should be held by member of staff and copied to line manager and CPD co-ordinator.

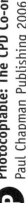 **Photocopiable: The CPD Co-ordinator's Toolkit**
Paul Chapman Publishing 2006 © Sue Kelly

Communicating your role

At around the same time that the initial CPD pro forma was introduced to staff, I was given the opportunity to 'set out my stall' to colleagues in my new role and to introduce or clarify what, for me, were the key principles of effective CPD. The most straightforward way of doing this initially, I felt, was to give a presentation to the teaching staff highlighting key issues in a clear way and at the same time challenging existing attitudes by exemplifying some new ideas for ways that we could move CPD forward.

The presentation is included here and in full on the CD-ROM (Figure 1.4) as a practical tool for other co-ordinators wishing to do the same. Although your school context and profile may be very different, hopefully all of you engaged with supporting the ongoing professional development of colleagues – whether it be in a small primary school, special school, secondary school or other institution where development is key to success – will be able to adapt, omit or insert additional slides to suit your specific purpose. You will note the reference to the DfES National Standards Framework, part of which has now been redrafted by the Teacher Development Agency. The subject leaders standards outlined here were not at the time of writing included in the redrafting process.

Using this presentation as a working model for producing your own will hopefully save busy CPD co-ordinators' time. The key elements of the presentation can be summarized as follows:

✓ making explicit the up-to-date role of the CPD co-ordinator

✓ identifying the range of possible developmental activities

✓ using the National Standards for middle leaders to begin to recognize their role in supporting and leading the CPD of those with whom they work (the same principle applies to any person who line manages or leads the work of individuals or teams whether it be in a secondary environment or not)

✓ at the same time as the above, making clear the need for individuals to be proactively engaged in their ongoing development

✓ promoting cost-effective, planned and imaginative approaches

✓ defining the role of the senior leadership team in supporting effective and consistent school practices

✓ demonstrating the need to link CPD to whole-school, departmental, pastoral or individual targets

✓ considering the impact of CPD on classroom practice.

Subsequent sections will explore in more detail each key element of the presentation and outline simple steps that can be taken to begin to effect real change in CPD culture. There will be supporting practical tools.

Figure 1.4   CPD – a vision (PowerPoint presentation slides)

Objectives of this presentation

➢ To provide a basis for discussion of CPD practice in the school

➢ To evaluate the content of this presentation in informing and supporting CPD practices at whole school/departmental/team level

➢ To outline future targets and dates for action

➢ To consider SLG involvement

a

Objectives of this presentation

➢ To raise the profile of CPD practices within the school

➢ To make explicit the role of the CPD co-ordinator

➢ To consider CPD practices at departmental/ faculty level

➢ To identify and discuss the relationship between CPD and Performance Review processes

b

CONTINUING PROFESSIONAL DEVELOPMENT

A VISION

c

My definition

CPD is … any activity which enhances the quality of teaching and learning within the school. It should develop the school and the individual and impact directly on what goes on in the classroom.

d

'Support for teachers' own learning and development is a key characteristic of the Intelligent School. This applies to individuals, to groups of teachers in year or department teams and to the whole school as an institution. In this context, the needs of individuals as well as the institution have to be acknowledged. Individual teachers need to be involved with whole school learning initiatives. They must also have the opportunity to fulfil their own personal and professional needs'.
(*The Intelligent School.* MacGilchrist, Myers, Reed)

e

Effective CPD

● **What it is:**
Effective CPD links school development planning, personal development and performance review processes.

● **What it is not:**
An ad-hoc process.
Effective CPD should be a part of all the above and developed from the above.

f

▶

Traditional v. modern view of CPD

The traditional role:
'… A deputy who looks after courses and things'

The up-to-date role:
'Taking the management of professional development a stage further than administration, beyond the bounds of matching courses to development plans and post-Ofsted action plans and into the realms of a fundamental re-think about what constitutes real professional development and how we realise an aspiration to facilitate it.'

g

So … what exactly is the role of the CPD co-ordinator?

What I think it is:

- To raise the profile of, facilitate, monitor and evaluate CPD practices within the school.

- To provide guidance to staff as they seek to participate in constructive developmental activity.

h

What my role is not:

1. One of control
2. To sign course application forms

i

Professional development should be centred on raising standards in the classroom and teachers should learn on the job and from the best.

Teachers' prime concerns are their subject knowledge and pedagogical skills and when individual teachers are asked about the development activities that have had most impact on their classroom practice they mainly mention the following:

- Opportunities to learn from and with other teachers, in their own or other schools
- Observing colleagues teaching and discussing what they have observed
- High-quality focused training on specific areas
- Taking part in coaching and mentoring partnerships

j

True or false?

Effective CPD only happens through people going on courses.

k

So how does effective CPD happen?

- ✓ Reflecting on what happens in lessons
- ✓ Asking pupils their opinions of lessons
- ✓ Inviting a colleague to observe a lesson
- ✓ Planning a lesson with a colleague
- ✓ Discussing pupils' work
- ✓ Coaching a colleague in an aspect of their work/being coached yourself
- ✓ Reading information, research, articles, journals, etc.
- ✓ Being a mentor/mentee
- ✓ Leading a staff meeting/Inset/contributing to a dept meeting
- ✓ Gaining accreditation (e.g. diploma, MA, vocational qualification, etc.)

How many more things can we add to this list?

l

▶

Subject leaders, HODS, other managers

- *What CPD practices can you identify within your department/subject area?*
- *How do you recognize these?*
- *What opportunities are you creating for professional development for staff you manage?*
- *Do you actively promote the need to identify CPD practices and the gathering of evidence to support where it has taken place?*

m

The National Standards for subject leaders ...

... Has a section which highlights our role in managing staff and other adults.
This states that we should:
'Lead professional development through example and support, and co-ordinate the provision of high quality professional development by methods such as coaching, drawing on other sources of expertise as necessary, for example higher education, LEAs and subject associations.'
Are we achieving this standard with regard to current managing of CPD practices in our departments/subject areas/faculties/teams?
If not, how can we do so?

n

What can we do to raise the profile of CPD within the school/at departmental level?

- Make explicit what CPD means and the role of CPD co-ordinator
- Provide the opportunity for leaders to begin to consider their role in leading CPD practices for their teams
- Make time for CPD to happen, e.g. in departmental/team meetings

o

One tiny step ...

A 15-minute departmental slot dedicated to CPD could include the following:

- ❖ 10-minute presentations of recent developments in a subject area on a rotational basis
- ❖ Feedback and identification of any staff development which has taken place (i.e. not just a course)
- ❖ Discussion of strategies to use with a particular group/pupil
- ❖ Development of departmental SOW
- ❖ Sharing of good practice

... and many more

p

SLG issues

Monitoring that CPD issues are being addressed at departmental/faculty/team level.
For example:

- ➤ That feedback to department following any CPD activity, takes places i.e.: through departmental minutes
- ➤ That middle leaders are actively managing and effectively leading CPD for their teams
- ➤ That feedback from performance reviews is recorded effectively in order to inform future planning at departmental/school levels
- ➤ That any CPD issues are fedback to CPD co-ordinator

q

Action plan

- Short term targets
  - To raise awareness of CPD practices already in existence across the school/in departments
  - To think about more effective ways of monitoring the impact of these on practice in the classroom/pupil performance
  - To use performance reviews/observation and monitoring of teaching and learning to more successfully inform future CPD
  - To engage the support of middle/team leaders, to facilitate practice and provide support for them in leading, managing and being responsible for CPD at departmental/team level

r

What is the question behind all CPD?

Answer:

What impact does professional development practice in the school have on teaching and learning in the classroom?

s

THE CPD MANTRA

'Learning from each other and learning from what works'

t

What next?

- Discussion of professional development needs at department/team level using the pro formas completed on the last Inset day
- CPD co-ordinator to use above to identify opportunities for professional development on an individual level and to highlight whole school issues
- Middle/team leaders to receive budget allocations in order to begin to identify and plan for professional development needs
- Staff to be consulted on CPD issues to be discussed, through setting up a CPD working party

u

Teachers' standards framework for threshold standard states that teachers should ...

... demonstrate responsibility for their professional development and use the outcomes to improve teaching and pupils' learning.

v

CPD in a vibrant learning community:

Look to the future ...

- That we all take responsibility for our own professional development and seek ways to enhance this

- That we acknowledge more actively the expertise of colleagues and value the use of this to support the CPD of each other on a daily basis

w

CPD in a vibrant learning community:

- That management of CPD at team levels is creative and explicit

- That CPD practices are focused and tailor made to meet performance review, departmental/other teams and whole-school targets i.e.: that they impact more directly on teaching and learning in the classroom

x

Supporting middle leaders or those outside the secondary phase who have responsibility for the CPD of individuals or teams

I once listened with admiration to a primary school CPD co-ordinator as she clearly and enthusiastically outlined her vision for CPD practices in her own school with 150 children on role and a staff of approximately 10. She concluded her presentation with the following statement: 'I have no idea how you could lead CPD practices in a large secondary school with so many staff!' She is not alone. This section will provide clear guidance for CPD co-ordinators in large schools or institutions for doing so – with a focus on the role of middle leaders within schools which have that structure. The National Standards Framework for teachers provides the basis for outlining the role of subject and pastoral leaders in leading CPD for the teams with which they are working. The same principle can be applied to those line managers of non-teaching and support staff who are also key in managing and co-ordinating planned developmental activities for those with whom they work closely. It is the entitlement of all the staff of any institution to have the opportunity to take part in planned developmental activity which will have a positive impact on their work, the work of their team/department and that of the establishment. In the case of the schools and colleges in which we are lucky enough to work, it is the work of *all* colleagues, not just the teaching staff, which contributes to the learning of the students in them. At the same time, we must all of us model effective learning practices for our students which will support them at school and throughout their future lives.

Having made explicit the responsibility of middle leaders/line managers in supporting and leading CPD for colleagues as stipulated in the National Standards, you are now in a good position to be able to guide and support this important work. It is through the work of these key members of staff that effective practice will develop and your responsibility now comes through the way you co-ordinate, challenge and engage these key professionals.

Some guidance for supporting the work of those who are responsible for leading and managing the CPD of others

The first key principle should be to ensure that all of those leading teams or individuals are aware of the need to ensure that any departmental, subject or team objectives need to support those of the whole-school development/improvement plan (SDP/SIP). These whole-school objectives will be driven by the School Evaluation Form (SEF) which provides the basis for Ofsted inspections and, with everyone in the school working towards them, will ensure that the school is in a position to drive standards forward and, as a consequence, that the pupils make good progress. A practical approach to targeting planned support to meet these identified needs is included in Chapter 2.

 Secondly, you may wish to use or adapt the two pro formas provided as Figures 1.5 and 1.6, in this case for subject and pastoral leaders, as a starting point to consider how more opportunities for CPD within those teams can be created. If nothing else, encouraging middle leaders to share the pro formas and use them as a basis for discussion of how CPD is led in their particular teams, should foster some healthy debate about where CPD practices are and need to go, while involving everybody in the process.

Figure 1.5   Creating CPD opportunities for subject teams pro forma

Are we creating enough opportunities for CPD at department/faculty/team level?

CPD activity	Do we do this?	Could we do this?	If so who would be involved?
Observing a colleague teach an area of expertise			
Visiting a school with a particular focus on an area of expertise and feeding back at a departmental/team meeting			
Coaching a colleague to teach an area of the SOW with which he/she may be unfamiliar			
Leading a departmental/team meeting			
Writing action points for a departmental meeting and setting the agenda in consultation with HOD/other colleagues			
Agreed peer observation, discussion of the process and delivery of feedback			
Mentoring a new member of staff and giving feedback of the experience to other colleagues			
Setting up a new extra-curricular club			
Networking with colleagues in the area with an agreed departmental/team focus			
Discussion of team teaching experience			
Sharing expertise in ICT at a departmental meeting			
Setting up a CPD notice board to display recent developments/articles of interest connected with your subject/area of work			

CPD activity	Do we do this?	Could we do this?	If so who would be involved?
Finding out about a new development within your subject and sharing with other colleagues			
Feeding back informally/more formally (e.g. handouts) on a course/other CPD activity to your colleagues			
Use of pupil feedback to evaluate individual/departmental practice			
Setting up a CPD library of relevant books on pedagogy, etc.			
Mentoring pupils and feeding back on the experience			
Sharing of good practice timetabled into a departmental/team meeting			

Other ideas for departmental/team CPD could include the following:

• • • • •

Figure 1.6 Creating CPD opportunities for pastoral teams pro forma

Are we creating enough opportunities for CPD at pastoral team level?

CPD activity	Do we do this?	Could we do this?	If so who would be involved?
Observing an experienced tutor in tutor time			
Visiting a school with a particular focus on an area of expertise such as behaviour management/peer counselling			
Leading a pastoral meeting			
Leading a departmental meeting			
Agreed peer observation, discussion of the process and delivery of feedback			
Mentoring a new tutor and giving feedback			
Discussion of team tutoring experiences			
Sharing expertise in ICT at a year group/pastoral team meeting with a focus on the use of this to enhance effective tutoring			
Setting up a CPD notice board to display recent developments/articles of interest connected with pastoral management			

CPD activity	Do we do this?	Could we do this?	If so who would be involved?
Feeding back informally/more formally (e.g. handouts) on a CPD activity to other tutors			
Setting up a CPD library of relevant books on issues			
Mentoring pupils and feeding back on the experience at a tutor meeting			
Sharing of good practice timetabled in a tutor meeting			

Other ideas for pastoral team/individual CPD could include the following:

- •
- •
- •
- •

Thirdly, continuing with your 'simple steps' approach to effecting a change of culture and with the support of your senior leadership team, request that leaders across the school take a fresh look at the way that they are leading meetings and ask them to reflect on whether or not these could be more developmental. In my school, middle leaders were asked to consider the agenda items of meetings and simply to put those items of a developmental nature under the heading of CPD. The thinking behind this was once again to raise the profile of CPD, to challenge the culture of not recognizing much of what we do as being developmental and of benefit to our practices, and at the same time to increase the 'feel good' factor among the staff as they began to realize a lot more training was happening than they had ever acknowledged in the past!

Finally, at this stage, I began to put together a questionnaire for later use, with the intention of challenging team leaders to reflect on the strengths and areas for development of individuals within their teams. Only by recognizing and being clear about the skills and knowledge of those individuals could leaders begin to deploy this expertise effectively throughout the team. In this way each member would have something to contribute to raising standards and developing consistency within the department for the benefit of staff and students alike.

Points to remember

- Begin to make explicit the role of middle leaders/line managers in leading the CPD of others.
- Request that, where appropriate, developmental agenda items are put under a CPD heading.
- Encourage teams to discuss CPD and how more opportunities can be created within them.
- Encourage leaders to consider how expertise within teams can be deployed more effectively.

You may find useful the following Teachers TV programmes:

Secondary CPD in Action: Sharing Skills
Primary CPD: 4 programmes to support your practices
Go to www.teachers.tv. Select "video library", then "secondary" and "headteacher/senior manager" options

CHAPTER 2

Developing a strategic approach to CPD practices

This chapter will move forward your strategic leadership of CPD in leaps and bounds. Using the individual staff development pro forma will build on the practices already in place as outlined in Chapter 1. The benefits of using the pro forma are made explicit for co-ordinators who, in turn, will need to articulate these clearly to staff. There are easy to follow sections on maximizing the use of the pro forma to support the work of middle and team leaders as they plan to meet targeted needs in a cost-effective way. The pro forma can be used to support your strategic approach as a busy CPD co-ordinator in meeting the identified needs of the whole school and individuals within it. Best practice principles such as cost-effective use of resources, encouraging staff towards a proactive engagement with their own ongoing development and imaginative approaches are integral to the processes outlined here.

Targeted use of resources – the individual staff development pro forma

The individual staff development pro forma to which you have already been introduced in 'prototype' form in Chapter 1, has been an essential tool in the development of ongoing CPD processes over the past three years in my school and is still a work in progress (Figure 2.1). I designed the pro forma with the help of my headteacher initially to support my own planning for CPD practices in the school and that of subject and pastoral leaders. However, the pro forma could easily be adapted to suit the specific context and needs of colleagues in your school including support staff. Chapter 3 provides a more detailed outline of the role of the CPD co-ordinator in

leading practices for this group of newly termed paraprofessionals. In the meantime, the pro forma could look like the example I have included in Figure 2.2.

Each member of staff completes the form yearly online, identifying a range of objectives, from classroom observation areas for development to performance review development targets. The main benefits of using the pro forma or a tool like it and the key elements of CPD good practice which it supports are, in my view, as follows:

Figure 2.1 Individual staff development pro forma

Member of staff: .... Department: .... Date: ....

Academic year 200X/200Y Please complete the indicated sections with your identified training needs	Identified needs from observations 1. 2.	ICT needs departmental/individual 1. 2.	Departmental targets for year 1. 2.	Targets from Performance Review 1. 2.	Date completed with evidence trail
In order to fulfil the identified targets above I could be involved in the following CPD activities: Please tick					
Observing good practitioners: Observing other teachers teaching					
Shadowing a colleague					
Visiting and seeing another school in action					
Observing and working with a visiting expert					
Extending professional experience: Leading and contributing to school-based Inset					
Rotation of roles/jobs					
Developing own professional profile					
Co-ordinating/managing a subject					
Assuming the role of leader for a special initiative in school					
Carrying out action research in the classroom/school					
Contributing to a professional publication					
Gaining experience of interviewing					
Acting as a performance reviewer					

23

Being reviewed				
Serving as a governor				
Serving on professional committee/working parties				
Becoming a union representative				
Leading/supervising non-professionals who work in the classroom				
Working on extra-curricular activities				
Taking part in staff conferences on individual pupils				
Working with other professionals such as education psychologists				
Working with an exam board or marking exam papers				
Networking and sharing with a group of colleagues from another school				
Team teaching				
Learning through professional practice with others				
Developing pedagogy in the context of ICT				
Peer mentoring, e.g. mentoring a NQT				
Organizing a display in collaboration with colleagues				
Working with pupils: Taking responsibility for a group of pupils on an off-site visit				
Developing teaching skills across a wide age and ability range				
Working with pupils on school councils				

Working with pupils to present an assembly, play, musical performance or other event				
Working with pupils preparing a school year book				
Collaborating with peripatetic teachers				
Mentoring individual pupils				
Taking time to evaluate your own practice: Inviting your peers to observe you				
Getting feedback from your own pupils				
Analyzing class and examination work				
Integrating the use of pupil websites and online communities into teaching				
Using e-mail/videoconferencing between pupils in teaching				
Negotiating targets and evaluating work alongside pupils				
Reviewing your marking				
Videoing yourself				
Other: In-house training: at departmental/whole school level				
ICT training in-house				
International exchange or visit				
Aspiring Leader Conference				
External/county courses				

A copy of this completed pro forma should be held by member of staff and copied to line manager and CPD co-ordinator.

Figure 2.2 Individual support staff development pro forma

Member of staff: .... Team: .... Line Manager: .... Date: ....

Please complete the indicated sections with your identified training needs:	Identified needs from appraisal 1. 2.	ICT team/individual needs 1. 2.	Other training needs	Date completed with evidence trail
Observing other colleagues:				
Shadowing a colleague				
Visiting and seeing another school in action				
Observing and working with a visiting expert/in-house expert/learning conversations with colleagues				
Extending on the job experience:				
Rotation of role/jobs				
Developing own job profile				
Co-ordinating/managing a project				
Assuming the role of leader for a special initiative in school/my team/other team				
Being reviewed/appraised				
Serving on a committee/working party				
Working on extra-curricular activities				
Networking and sharing with a group of colleagues from another school				
Other:				
Leading or participating in a training activity for either support or teaching staff				
ICT training in-house				
External/county courses				

A copy of this completed pro forma should be held by member of staff, line manager and a copy passed to CPD co-ordinator.

Photocopiable: The CPD Co-ordinator's Toolkit
Paul Chapman Publishing 2006 © Sue Kelly

✓ A range of professional objectives are kept 'live' for staff.

✓ Colleagues can refer to and update the pro forma with completion dates for specific objectives and get a real sense that they are moving forward in areas of their development.

✓ Staff can be encouraged to record, or at least consider, where the evidence for completion of an objective or part of an objective, can be found. This supports the collation of evidence for performance reviews, particularly those related to pay progression.

✓ By selecting one or two CPD activities in which they would like to participate to support their ongoing development in these specified areas, staff are effectively making a choice about their preferred 'learning style' to do so.

✓ By considering a whole range of possible CPD activities, staff are constantly reminded of the myriad nature of activities which constitute effective CPD as discussed in Chapter 1.

✓ Following on from the above, participation in many of these activities, which will undoubtedly have a positive impact on classroom practice or other important areas of our work, will be far more cost-effective and relevant to immediate needs than attending an external course.

✓ The whole process encourages staff to be proactive in their approach to their own development and discourages a mindset of CPD being something that somebody else does or organizes for them.

✓ The completion of the pro forma supports planning and monitoring practices at every level within the school including that of the work of the CPD co-ordinator, examples of which will be related later on in this chapter.

Once colleagues have completed the pro forma they are requested to forward a copy to me as CPD co-ordinator and to their subject leader/head of department/team leader. This provides vital information which can then inform yearly CPD planning. The emphasis is on an imaginative, cost-effective approach which *targets* support to the needs of the school, teams within the school and individual staff.

Some work may need to be done beforehand to advise and guide staff as to how best to complete the pro forma. It is worth spending some time here to consider the objective headings so that you can ensure that staff are clear what the expectations of each are.

Areas for development from observations

Given the huge amount of resources which are expended in the process of observing colleagues and the considerable developmental potential for individuals if carried out successfully, it would seem to make sense to record any outcomes for further development on the pro forma so that these can be planned for. Any development of skills should then, without any doubt if thoughtfully provided, have a direct impact on classroom practice. This will impact on students' learning and the progress they make, on the skills and confidence of the teacher and the work of others if shared across the team, the school and, if possible, among colleagues in other schools.

By keeping areas for development 'live' on the pro forma in this way, teachers or other colleagues can focus on specific areas of their work. How many of us read and discuss the feedback following an observation, fully intend to work on that area of our practice and either lose the impetus to work on our targets once back in the classroom or quite simply forget what they were.

ICT individual or team targets

There are few of us in the profession who feel that we have nothing to learn in terms of improving our information and communications technology (ICT) skills. What is more, if we are to equip our students successfully for the rapidly advancing technological world in which they will live, then quite frankly we are doing them a huge disservice if we do not make improving our own skills a priority. Many of us remember the Learning Skills Council drive a few years ago to improve the ICT skills of the teaching profession through New Opportunities Fund (NOF) accreditation. Although some of us may have scoffed at this thrust and the materials through which to gain accreditation at the time, there is still much to learn from the rationale behind the process. It is not only the need to develop our skills with specific programs and systems which is important. There is much for us to learn in successfully applying this knowledge and skills to the delivery of our subjects or learning objectives in whichever phase of education we may be working. The positive engagement of pupils through skilled use of ICT, as we all know, impacts not only on their learning but also on behaviour. That is why it is included here on the pro forma.

Departmental/pastoral/other team objectives

These will usually have been identified in the light of whole-school objectives outlined on the SIP. Leaders should be encouraged to plan to meet these on the yearly planner. Including them on the pro forma keeps them 'live' and a priority for the whole department/team. If staff forget what they are, then how can they support the work of the team in meeting them and, what is more, how can we ensure that they are in a position to support the identified objectives of the school?

Objectives identified during the process of performance review

Effective and challenging performance review procedures should now be in existence in every school across the country. If carried out skilfully then one of the outcomes of this process should be to identify training and further development needs for individuals with which they should be supported in their future work. It may be that immediate line managers/middle leaders can plan to support individuals to meet these needs on the annual planner. However, some of these developmental objectives may be of a confidential or sensitive nature, in which case staff should not feel pressured to include them on the pro forma but should be encouraged or advised to discuss them separately with either the CPD co-ordinator or a professional mentor of their choice.

Once middle/team leaders have a copy of the pro forma from each member of their department/team, your role as co-ordinator will be to advise them how best to use this information to prepare their annual plan for CPD. When supporting their work you will need to make them aware of the following:

✓ A departmental/team annual planner can be used and then shared with the team if this is appropriate – an exemplar is available for you to consider (Figure 2.3) which you can adapt to your purpose.

✓ Any allocated budget should be spread fairly across the team/department or at least taken into consideration.

✓ Planned CPD activities should take into account the learning choice preferences highlighted on the pro forma by individuals.

Figure 2.3 Departmental/team annual CPD planner

CPD planner 200X/200Y

Department ....

Budget ....

Identified target(s)	CPD activities	Staff	Estimated cost	Date	Success criteria	Feedback When? How?
Departmental (taken from department/ faculty action plan)						
Individual (taken from CPD pro formas)						

✓ Every team member should be included on the team plan with target dates specified for completion.

✓ Departmental meeting time should include *planned* CPD activities at given points through the year to address generic needs thrown up through the pro formas. This may be planned ICT training for the department to be delivered by the ICT co-ordinator, and so on, which needs to be built in well in advance.

✓ Effective dissemination and feedback of learning outcomes should be allowed for in department/team meetings. There should be an expectation that everybody feed back at least twice in a formal way with written outcomes/handouts and so on. This is excellent CPD for the whole team including the person leading this part of a meeting.

✓ The possible impact of selected CPD activities included on the yearly planner, should be discussed and recorded *beforehand* with team leaders/line managers. A learning log or journal can be used to record the key learning outcomes of more informal CPD and the impact of this on classroom practice. The impact of more formal and specific CPD activities, such as those outlined on the team planner taken from the staff development pro forma, should be considered beforehand as outlined in more detail in Chapter 6. This can then become the focus for discussion in subsequent meetings either on an individual or team basis, when the outcomes have been tried and tested in the classroom

Points to remember

- Guide and support staff to complete the pro forma appropriately.
- Be confident you are clear about the rationale behind it and how it supports effective CPD practices in order to sell the benefits to colleagues.
- Be prepared to spend time with middle/team leaders with annual planning based on the pro formas.
- Disseminate and share good practice from the above.

How the CPD pro forma can be used to aid the planning and development work of the CPD co-ordinator

Planning for departmental/team-led Inset time

Well planned, relevant and enjoyable use of whole-school Inset time can provide an enormous challenge for even the most experienced CPD co-ordinator. The staff of any school or educational institution brings with it diverse skills, areas of professional expertise, in and out of an educational environment, plus a wide range of experiences in the workplace. It can be an anxious time for co-ordinators as we desperately try to match the provision of Inset time to the needs of a large number of discerning professionals. Add to this the desire of most, if not all, conscientious CPD co-ordinators to provide value for money and to lead the way in modelling fundamental principles of effective CPD at the same time (that is, practising what we preach!), and it is not difficult to understand why a forthcoming Inset day can seriously affect the sleep patterns of even the most robust CPD leaders.

Using the individual staff development pro forma as a basis for planning can happen in a variety of ways. The complaint of many staff in my school has often been that insufficient time is set aside for professional development, and this may be a familiar tune in your own school. Having said that, in the early days of my role I began to suspect that perhaps the use of team meeting time on Inset days could be spent more imaginatively and with more focus on development rather than administration. By referring middle leaders to the information outlined on their team's returned pro formas, we can be more confident that departmental or other team-led Inset time is used more profitably to support the objectives identified. It can be exciting to see middle leaders putting together a day of CPD activities which match a range of individual, departmental and whole-school targets. What is more, the feeling among colleagues is more likely to be that their requests for more time for staff development have been listened to and, from a co-ordinator's point of view, colleagues will now be in a position to use the time more effectively. Our role from then on is to support and encourage heads of department and subject leaders to plan effectively for the day or time available. It is advisable to request an agenda well in advance as this will give you the opportunity to plan effectively and to guide, coach and, in some cases, help colleagues to come up with ideas. This approach has been a shift in my own school and the feedback from these days is always extremely positive, with staff engaged in a wide range of CPD activities. These often tap into existing departmental expertise, and opportunities are spread more fairly among departmental/team members. What is more, staff agree that the days are usually far more relevant to their immediate individual and departmental needs.

With this type of planned and focused approach you should by now be moving well away from the reality of demoralized staff measuring their worth by how many external courses they have been 'allowed' to go on. You should find that your role as co-ordinator is becoming far better understood. The role of the up-to-date CPD co-ordinator is no longer the traditional one of the 'deputy who signs course forms'. You should be aware of your role as truly becoming a facilitator and supporter of CPD practices in your school and, hopefully, it will feel very good!

Using the individual staff development pro forma to support the cost-effective use of whole-school Inset time

The first time I used the pro formas to inform my planning for Inset time, it became apparent that many staff felt the need to improve their range of strategies to manage pupil behaviour. As this was very much on the agenda of the National Strategy at the time, it seemed sensible to base a day of development training on that. After getting the go-ahead from my headteacher, I hunted about for an external provider on this occasion to lead the day for staff. With cost-effectiveness in mind, we decided to invite other local schools to join us on the day or to send groups of staff or individual staff if they wished to do so. Given that external providers can be pricey, this had an obvious benefit in sharing the cost but also seemed an ideal opportunity for staff to network with other schools and, hopefully, to establish some longer-term professional partnerships. A local mixed school with which we had shamefully little professional contact on a sustained or broad basis decided to send all of their staff, as did a local sixth form college. Here was an additional CPD opportunity for staff not to be missed! In an act of what I allowed myself to consider extreme cunning, but which in fact was just good common sense, I took the following steps to ensure that maximum benefit was derived from the day and that it suited the needs of the schools and staff involved:

- ✓ I made sure that our staff, including the Senior leadership Group (SLG), and the other schools involved had the opportunity to make explicit what they wanted from the day.

- ✓ I sent this information to the speaker well in advance in order to make clear our expectations and to provide him with a clear brief.

- ✓ In addition to the speaker's materials, I translated our brief into explicit aims and objectives for the day together with a series of clear learning outcomes, which were given to each member of staff.

- ✓ I asked a kind-hearted member of the design and technology (DT) department to make a series of easily visible signposts for every subject or department. These were put on the tables at lunchtime and staff were requested to sit with colleagues from other schools according to their teaching subject, in order to encourage networking, that is, no sitting with friends!

- ✓ All staff had been requested in advance to wear a name badge with their first name and surname clearly shown.

- ✓ I organized outside caterers to provide a buffet lunch. Again, all of these costs were shared.

You can be forgiven for thinking that I had gone completely mad organizing the Inset day for not one school but three, and I can assure you that the lead-up to the day was not without moments of (controlled) stress and anxiety! However, attention to detail in the planning and the help of some tremendous support staff (administrators and caretakers) ensured that everything went without a hitch. The feedback from staff was extremely positive and, although we had been expected to listen for much of the day, it was agreed that everyone had taken away several key strategies which could be used straight away in the classroom. It was also apparent that individual and groups of staff had organized visits and meetings with colleagues from other schools to discuss all kinds of professional and subject issues. My cunning networking plan had worked!

Embedding development training

The next step following any development training is to ensure that what we have all gained from the day is not immediately lost or forgotten. I am sure that most CPD co-ordinators have experienced the frustration of valuable development training disappearing all too soon into a distant memory of 'What did we do last Inset day? It was really good but I can't remember much about it'. I have found that embedding development training and monitoring the impact of it in any meaningful way is a tremendous challenge. I can only offer some generic strategies that I have used to keep the training 'live' and to try to ensure that our students benefit from any newly developed skills, improved understanding or renewed motivation.

- ✓ To embed any new skills requires a serious commitment of time and energy from us as co-ordinators; if we forget past development training and move on to the next Inset day, then so will staff.

✓ Give staff time on the day, in a plenary session, to write down one or two things which they will commit to trying out in the classroom on their first day back after the training session. Then ask for feedback.

✓ Through middle leaders (if a large school, or yourself if not) request that time is set aside in meetings for staff feedback and discussion of how the development training has impacted on their classroom practice over a period of time. This may be, for example, which strategies or skills have been most successful in a particular context. Collate this information and present it back to departments (or the whole staff in a smaller context) as a whole-school overview.

✓ In the case of specific strategies and techniques developed through training, use whole-school feedback to determine those which have had the most success and suggest to your SLG that these be incorporated into whole-school practices and procedures.

✓ Depending on the nature of the training and what staff have gained from it, encourage every department or faculty to provide evidence of impact in their area (all members of these teams should be expected to contribute). This can, in turn, be collated into a whole-school portfolio for all staff to consult.

✓ Give staff opportunities to share good practice on other Inset days in order to keep past training 'live'.

Planning to support the needs of individuals and the school – a cost-effective approach

Although much of the planned provision to meet staff needs should be led by team leaders, quite often colleagues will identify other objectives, which middle leaders may not be in a position to support. With some careful crafting and planning, not only can we help individual colleagues to achieve their targets but, at the same time, model excellent CPD practices, as befits our role and vision.

One practical example of this which could easily be adapted to fit a variety of circumstances, came about in the early days of my role. A fellow colleague had identified as a key CPD objective that he would like the opportunity to give a presentation to middle leaders at a development meeting. At the same time I had come across the details of what looked like a very interesting external course on raising the achievement of pupils performing marginally at GCSE. I immediately recognized the benefits to all staff of gaining some practical examples of tips to support the strategies we use to engage *all* pupils, with the possibility of improving our five A* to C percentage at GCSE at the same time.

I approached the member of staff concerned and asked if he would like to attend the course, which I would fund from the whole-school staff development allocation. The condition would be that he should then prepare a presentation for the middle leaders' group in order that any learning outcomes could be shared with department teams and benefit the whole of the teaching staff. He readily agreed and was delighted at the opportunity to gain this type of experience which he felt was a valuable asset to his professional portfolio. In fact, as I thought through the possible outcomes still further, I realized there was huge potential to disseminate the course outcomes across the whole school. I took the following steps to ensure that the teaching strategies he brought back with him from the course became embedded in practice across every department, with students on the receiving end of even more creative and engaging strategies to progress their learning:

✓ The member of staff attended the course and gave an excellent presentation of the outcomes to our middle leadership development group facilitated by me.

✓ A toolkit of activities to engage students of all learning styles and which could be adapted across the range of subjects was distributed to every teacher in the school.

✓ Working through heads of department, each member of staff was requested to trial at least three of the activities in their own classroom and to record the impact on learning on a prepared pro forma.

✓ Heads of department were asked to commit a meeting slot to sharing the outcomes of the classroom trials, with every member of the department feeding back on the strengths and weaknesses of the new activities.

✓ The feedback outlined above was collated and sent to me. Many of the activities had given a new momentum to classroom practice, particularly in adapting to the needs of visual and kinaesthetic learners. I asked each department to provide me with evidence of the impact on students' learning and created a portfolio of the outcomes.

Some departments went on to include the newly tried and tested activities and strategies in their revised schemes of work. For the cost of one external course and a bit of creative thinking, the impact of new learning and skills was felt in every classroom in the school, to the benefit of our students. At the same time, the whole process gave me the opportunity to model some best practice principles as CPD co-ordinator and to demonstrate to staff that I was able to practise what I was preaching.

Points to remember

- Support and guide middle leaders/line managers to plan to meet the needs of their teams using the planner.
- Ensure that middle leaders work to the principles of cost-effectiveness and equity of provision while encouraging staff to proactively engage in the process.
- Base any whole-school Inset provision on the generic outcomes of the individual staff development pro forma to ensure resources are targeted at identified needs.
- Support individuals to meet their identified development targets in a creative way.

CHAPTER 3

Supporting the needs of individuals and groups of individuals in your school

This chapter turns your attention towards the National Standards which have recently been redrafted and exemplified in the areas of Qualified Teacher status (QTS), induction, Senior Teacher/threshold, the introduction of Excellent Teacher status and the revised Advanced Skills Teacher status. Guidance is given on how to exploit the standards for the benefit of ongoing staff development and the career progression of teachers. This chapter also provides many practical tools to support the effective and successful induction year of newly qualified staff. The onus is on induction tutors to model exemplary professional standards and practices throughout this process; there is much to support them and give them confidence in this chapter to carry out efficiently and effectively what really is a crucial role within the school. Finally, the needs of support staff in school and the role of the CPD co-ordinator in developing these paraprofessionals are both given consideration.

If you have followed the advice in the previous chapters and tried out some of the activities suggested, then you should be well on your way towards developing the CPD practices in your school in line with the principles of best practice outlined by the DfES in their guidance document, *Leading and Coordinating CPD in Secondary Schools* (January 2005).

The guidance makes clear the government's focus on staff development as one of its five key principles of the Five Year Strategy for Children and Learners and refers to what it terms 'a new teacher professionalism' which carries with it 'implications for CPD in schools and beyond'. It goes on to make explicit that these changes will involve 'career progression and financial rewards going to those who are making the biggest contributions to improving pupil attainment, those who are continually developing their own expertise and those who help to develop expertise in other teachers'. The emphasis is on the use of the National Standards Framework, part of which is being redrafted at the moment and which is based on four main stages in the career ladder for teachers: those crossing the pay 'threshold' by getting Senior Teacher status; pay progression for senior teachers based on pay progression through the upper pay scale; the chance to work towards Excellent Teacher status for the most experienced classroom teachers; and more teachers applying for Advanced Skills Teacher posts.

Your work so far in developing a more focused and imaginative approach to CPD practices will support the DfES best practice principles and the standards criteria for the career stages outlined above, in the following ways:

- ✓ creating a positive working environment for staff

- ✓ building collaborative approaches to CPD

- ✓ establishing a *learning from each other* ethos

- ✓ promoting opportunities for teachers and support staff to develop expertise in others

- ✓ challenging mindsets about what activities constitute effective CPD

- ✓ considering the benefits of coaching and mentoring models of CPD

- ✓ considering the value of action research and development approaches

- ✓ inspiring innovative and imaginative approaches

- ✓ changing passive approaches to professional development to those which encourage a proactive engagement with the process

- ✓ promoting cost-effective, targeted approaches to the management and leadership of CPD

- ✓ modelling best practice for other leaders

- ✓ considering the impact of development activities on pupil attainment and achievement

- ✓ facilitating and supporting the work of other leaders in managing CPD for their teams

- ✓ supporting line managers to know their teams well enough to be able to deploy expertise to meet the existing needs of the team and the individuals within it

- ✓ encouraging networking and collaboration within and beyond the school community

- ✓ embedding the improvements into existing school systems

- ✓ creating a learning environment in your school – one where all staff model effective learning practices for students.

Practical approaches to some of these best practice principles will be further examined in subsequent chapters/sections.

The current standards framework can provide CPD co-ordinators with a valuable resource when supporting the needs of individuals and teams within the school to impact on whole-school improvement. 'The framework shows at a glance how the expectations of teachers can grow and change at different stages of a career as they take on different roles within the school. It should help people to recognize existing expertise and achievements as well as any developmental needs' (Earley and Bubb, *Leading and Managing CPD*, 2004: 30–1).

Using the standards to support individuals

The standards can be used in a variety of ways:

1. To help staff to recognize where they are meeting the criteria at a particular stage in their career and to identify areas of focus which can be included on their individual staff development pro forma (Chapter 2) as objectives/professional targets.

2. To support staff to plan in advance their future professional development needs in order to achieve a professional goal/career aspiration within a given timeframe.

3. To consider in advance the learning outcomes of a professional activity and the contribution it will make to career progression, the learning of students and the development of others in their team/school.

4. To consider in advance the nature and type of evidence to be gathered and which will support career progression through performance review systems in place in the school.

5. Through active engagement in the processes outlined above, to enable teachers to demonstrate explicitly a proactive involvement in their ongoing professional development which underpins the government's *New Teacher Professionalism* agenda.

Our role, then, as co-ordinators in schools and educational institutions becomes one of supporter and facilitator of these processes in order to ensure that staff are sufficiently prepared to progress successfully. One approach to consider when supporting individuals' career progression is to promote the standards and actively employ them to help teachers to identify explicit professional aims and objectives. Adapting the standards as a useful self-evaluation pack can be done easily. By judging progress against a five-point scale teachers can gauge to what extent they are meeting each of the criteria. Each strand of the criteria could be inserted into a table as illustrated below using one element of the Threshold criteria in the area of Managing Own Performance and Development.

Managing Own Performance and Development	5	4	3	2	1	Evidence for this
Teachers demonstrate responsibility for their professional development and use the outcomes to improve teaching and pupil learning						

Key:
1. I know I meet this criteria.

2. I largely meet this criteria.

3. I partly meet this criteria.

4. I need to improve in this aspect of my work.

5. I am unable to meet this criteria at the moment.

In this way teachers can be actively engaged in the process of self-evaluation of their progress towards the standards relevant to their career stage. Working with the CPD co-ordinator, team leader or line manager, individuals can began to identify strengths and weaknesses by judging themselves against the criteria and by doing so to tease out areas for focus which can be included on the individual staff development pro forma outlined in Chapter 2. Similarly, newly qualified staff can gauge their progress towards the induction standards and, with the support of the professional tutor, be engaged in the process of setting termly objectives to ensure they keep on track for the induction year. Current or aspiring middle leaders can use the self-evaluation materials to identify explicit professional targets to support their development in their current role or in a role to which they aspire.

Building a professional portfolio

Initially in my role I found many staff reluctant to consider putting together a professional development portfolio. From a personal point of view I found the negative attitude of some staff a bit perplexing and demotivating. It always helps in these situations to have an idea of where the opposition comes from. Quite often, as teachers, we oppose change because we fear it, and it soon became clear that many staff simply lacked the confidence to consider collecting the evidence for a portfolio or felt that they did not have the time to invest in it in view of all the other demands of the job. I started by outlining the benefits of developing a portfolio, by overcoming the opposing arguments and by putting forward some ideas about what a portfolio could look like – although this is really up to the individual. The presentation slides I have included here and on the CD-ROM (Figure 3.1) could be adapted for any situation where compiling a professional portfolio is desirable. I enhanced this desirability by throwing in a freebie document wallet for every member of staff – always a good selling technique, and money well spent from my limited staff development budget. It did indeed get the ball rolling!

Points to remember:

- Refer to the National Standards Framework and make staff aware of them.
- Encourage staff to use the standards to identify areas for professional development in order to support ongoing development or career aspirations – these can be recorded on the pro forma and aid planning for these specific needs.
- Develop models of self-review like the one here and use them to facilitate ongoing CPD practices.
- Encourage staff to develop an ongoing professional development portfolio which supports career progression against the National Standards.

Supporting newly qualified teachers in your school

One of the fundamental principles to remember when supporting newly qualified teachers (NQTs) to progress through the induction year successfully, is that all new members of the profession have an *entitlement* to a well planned and professionally delivered first year in the classroom. With this principle firmly in mind it is difficult for induction tutors to go wrong. What is also exciting from a CPD perspective is that the whole of the induction year is underpinned by

Figure 3.1   Developing a professional portfolio – why bother?
(PowerPoint presentation slides)

A professional development record/portfolio

Why bother?

a

Common questions

- What exactly is it?
- Why do I need one?
- What do I put in it?
- When will I have the time to do one?
- Where do I start?
- Do I have to use a computer?

b

What exactly is it?

'A confidential and voluntary collection of material that records and reflects upon an individual's work ... Pupils' work is at the heart of evidence collection. The individual needs to amass a tangible way of showing that s/he is developing as a professional educator.'

c

Why do I need one?

It can help you to prepare evidence for:

- A job interview
- A Threshold, Excellent or Advanced Skills teacher (AST) application
- A performance review meeting
- Possible accreditation of learning

d

Why do I need one?

It can help you to plan your career by:

- Collecting evidence of your current achievements, skills and attributes
- Recording your career history including prior work experience
- Reflecting on your teaching and learning and setting objectives for personal improvement

e

Why do I need one?

It can help you to plan your learning and development by:

- Analysing your strengths as a teacher and areas for further development
- Identifying and targeting learning and development opportunities
- Identifying appropriate qualifications

f

▶

And also because ...

☺ ... there are strong 'good practice' pressures filtering down from the DfES

☺ In itself it provides excellent evidence of a proactive engagement with, and commitment to, the process of your own continuing professional development

g

What do I put in it?

Any evidence of your achievements and experiences, for example:

✓ Certificates and qualifications
✓ Relevant external or internal Inset attended
✓ Posts held
✓ Particular responsibilities
✓ Skills in areas such as team building, working together and motivating others
✓ Your own learning, development and experiences as they happen
✓ Other relevant experience or attributes

h

But I haven't had any professional development this year as I haven't been on any courses ...

Examples of CPD other than external courses:

❑ Observing good practitioners
❑ Extending professional experience
❑ Working with pupils
❑ Taking time to evaluate your own practice
❑ Consult your individual staff development pro forma for the range of opportunities available

i

When will I have the time to do one?

> You're already doing one – you just need to collect the evidence
> It's a continual process – add to it as you go along

j

Where do I start?

● Gather evidence of your achievements – this could be in the form of photographs, letters, reports, lesson plans, minutes or outcomes of meetings, observation feedback, videotapes, certificates etc
● Think about what you have learnt from these achievements
● Reflect on your current practice
● Decide what you want to achieve and set objectives
● Record these on your individual staff development pro forma in discussion with your team leader
● Consider the success criteria, timeframes and possible impact of meeting your objectives
● What evidence will reflect successful completion of these and where will it be found?

k

Do I have to use a computer?

Up to you!

l

Photocopiable: The CPD Co-ordinator's Toolkit
Paul Chapman Publishing 2006 © Sue Kelly

ongoing development practices which will benefit not only new colleagues, but also open up rich opportunities for more experienced teachers to take on new responsibilities and the learning which these bring with them. At the same time, mentors of newly qualified colleagues can obtain the following additional benefits from involvement in the year:

✓ They can demonstrate a commitment to the professional development of others as outlined in the standards for the new Excellent Teacher status and also towards meeting the criteria for Advanced Skills status.

✓ They can show a proactive engagement with their own professional development and experience the privileges of guiding and shaping the practices of those who will be entertaining and educating children in classrooms long after we have retired to our pied a terre in France!

You may find it useful at this point to refer to the differences between the roles of mentor and coach which are outlined in Chapter 4.

It is important then for the induction tutor – often the CPD co-ordinator in a school or educational institution – to be clear about the CPD opportunities on offer for all those who are involved in the induction programme. I have outlined these in Figures 3.2 and 3.3 which you may wish to share not just with NQTs but also with subject mentors or any colleague in the school who will play a part in supporting our new colleagues to meet successfully the induction standard requirements. Once all colleagues can see the learning benefits not only for newly qualified colleagues but also for themselves, you may find that the whole idea of mentoring an NQT becomes quite an exciting prospect!

It is so easy as an experienced member of staff to see ourselves in the position of teacher/ expert when working with colleagues who are just embarking on their careers. This perspective can result in mentors feeling 'put upon' by having to support new staff, and this resentment at having another 'job to do' can easily affect relationships and sour what should be an exciting and stimulating first year of teaching for mentees. What is more, such an attitude can blind us to just how much we can learn from new colleagues. Acknowledging the relationship of mentor and new teacher as being mutually beneficial in terms of what each can gain from the other and which can then support the work of other colleagues in department teams and beyond, can prove a confidence boost for new staff and provide a fresh lease of life for existing teachers. It is our job as co-ordinators/induction tutors to shape staff thinking and to change old-fashioned attitudes towards the induction of new staff, should these be harmful or diminishing in any way. We should also recognize and value the induction process for the rich learning opportunities which it affords us as induction tutors!

So much has already been written to guide induction tutors and to ensure that we meet the statutory requirements of the year that it would be unnecessary to do so here. Sara Bubb's book entitled *Helping Teachers Develop* has a particularly useful chapter on observation procedures and rightly identifies observation as a *powerful tool for assessing and monitoring a teacher's practice* and as *a way to support teachers, because observation gives such a detailed picture and enables very specific objectives to be set.* Bubb's chapter has many practical and helpful tips to guide teachers through a successful observation process which is a very important part of any teacher's professional development and integral to the progress of newly qualified staff in their first year. Chapter 5 considers the processes and procedures of observation with an emphasis on using this as a key tool for developing classroom practice. The following sections of this chapter will provide other practical tips and guidance for busy induction tutors who

Figure 3.2   NQT induction programme: CPD for mentors

✓   Introductory session with CPD co-ordinator/induction tutor to establish the key requirements for the year. Important aspects of the programme outlined and explained, for example an introduction to the induction standards, remission time and use of, overview of requirements including the review and assessment meetings structure.

✓   Sharing of good practice. Experienced mentors share top tips with new mentors, e.g. ideas for effective use of ongoing meetings and the kind of support needed at particular points through the year.

✓   Individual coaching partnerships established to pair up experienced/less experienced or new subject mentors.

✓   Ongoing support from induction tutor via memos, e-mails, informal catch-up sessions.

✓   Copy of all e-mails/agendas for NQT meetings and other materials issued to NQTs sent to subject mentors also.

✓   Subject mentors involved directly in the assessment process – required to draft statements against the induction standards which are merged with CPD co-ordinator's and which are then agreed.

✓   Subject mentors invited to final presentation meeting when NQTs give a presentation on an interesting pedagogical issue related to their subject. Good CPD for mentors to keep abreast of new or recent developments in the delivery of their subject.

✓   Subject mentors asked to reflect on the experience of mentoring a newly qualified colleague and what they have learned from the process. This is fed back to the induction tutor, crystallizes the learning outcomes for them and is valuable CPD if fed back to other colleagues who may be keen to mentor an NQT in the future.

A review of the above is carried out annually with suggestions from all of those involved in the process. Feedback is used to refine and improve planning for the following year.

 Photocopiable: The CPD Co-ordinator's Toolkit
Paul Chapman Publishing 2006 © Sue Kelly

Figure 3.3   NQT induction programme: CPD for NQTs

✓ Career Entry Development Profile (CEDP) used to ensure continuity and progression of professional objectives initially.

✓ NQTs attend induction programme for all new staff in the autumn term which covers a range of issues and topics.

✓ Regular meetings set up with pastoral/subject leader/mentor. Induction tutor receives action points from these.

✓ Action plan review meetings with induction tutor to review progress against the standards.

✓ Articles of interest passed to NQTs for comments and discussion.

✓ NQT CPD section in library for NQTs to use, review and add to.

✓ NQTs to feedback ongoing development activities and learning outcomes to other team members at meetings. Excellent CPD for NQTs and other colleagues.

✓ Attendance at external county training and networking schemes. Learning outcomes recorded in ongoing learning journal and fed back to CPD co-ordinator and relevant colleagues.

✓ Regular self-review against the induction standards to evaluate progress.

✓ NQTs record outcomes of key meetings at review and assessment points in the year. Encourages a proactive engagement with the induction process and informs induction tutor of level of understanding of processes and procedures.

✓ NQTs meet with induction tutor as a group from spring term onwards. NQTs set the agenda – induction tutor facilitates ongoing CPD, supports and guides.

✓ NQTs visit another school(s) with an agreed focus linked to the induction standards and their personal objectives. Written feedback to induction tutor and other colleagues in department/team.

✓ NQTs present on a recent development in their subject/aspect of pedagogy/recent development in the use of ICT etc. Encourages new colleagues to research, read current journals, keep abreast of issues relevant to them. This also fosters a proactive engagement with the process and provides an important CPD opportunity to give a presentation to other staff.

✓ NQTs requested to carry out peer observations within their department/team and also to observe each other and give feedback on an agreed focus.

✓ NQTS observed regularly throughout the year. Focused feedback provides excellent support and guidance for future professional development objectives.

take their role seriously and are intent on giving new teachers the best possible start to their careers.

What is the role of the induction tutor?

Formally the person chosen as induction tutor should meet the criteria in Figure 3.4. Use this simple checklist to identify where you feel confident in your role and where you feel that you yourself need extra support, training or guidance.

On a day-to-day basis I believe it is crucial that as induction tutors we meet the professional standards listed in Figure 3.5.

Much of the rest of this section will quite simply consist of some practical examples of action plans, sample meeting agendas, memos, and so on, which as a busy co-ordinator/induction tutor you will be able to use straight away and adapt to your own needs. You will also find them useful in order to meet the very high professional standards you have set yourself when considering the checklist in Figure 3.5.

Developing an effective induction programme for all staff new to your school, institution or workplace

Involve newly qualified colleagues fully in the general induction programme for your school, which will probably include sending out key information before any new colleague takes up his/her post. Most schools and institutions have well-planned induction programmes for new colleagues. In my school this involves the following:

- ✓ sending out a welcome letter with key information enclosed (see exemplar in Figure 3.6)

- ✓ providing each member of staff with a welcome induction booklet with key information about school procedures, meeting times, key personnel, timings of the school day, and so on

- ✓ sending out a copy of the induction programme for all staff new to the school (see exemplar in Figure 3.7)

- ✓ offering new staff the opportunity to have a 'buddy mentor' in school either within or outside of their department/faculty with whom they can consult informally throughout their first year (see exemplar memo for existing staff, in Figure 3.8).

Given that rigorous induction procedures are essential in supporting new staff to get on top of a school's or other institution's systems and fundamental to their ability to function as effectively and quickly as possible in the classroom with students, do not feel apologetic or uncomfortable about your school's expectations in respect of participation in such a programme. Keep the programme dynamic by evaluating it on a yearly basis with new staff so that you can be sure it meets current needs. Encourage both support staff and teaching staff to participate in it, for example, to buddy mentor new colleagues and adapt the timetable of induction to ensure it meets the needs of both teaching and support staff by involving appropriate colleagues to deliver it.

Figure 3.4   NQT induction tutor checklist – formal procedures

Criteria	Confident I do this/ know this: Y/N	I need further support and guidance in these areas (outline what you feel they are)	Action to be taken and by whom
The up-to-date National Standards are my reference point and used as a focus for the year. I am clear about the standards for the award of QTS and the Induction Standards			
I feel I have been suitably trained for the role and understand the key aspects			
I use the Career Entry Profile as a starting point for initial action planning to ensure effective transition from NQT training to induction year			
10% remission time has been built into the NQTs' timetable. This is identified on the timetable, used for ongoing development activities only and NQTs have been requested to log use of this time			
I know how to ensure that the induction programme meets the specific individual needs of each NQT			
I know exactly what to do if I feel an NQT is failing to achieve the standards			
I have a structured programme for the year which has been shared with all those involved. Regular observation has been built into the programme at least twice a term			

45

Criteria	Confident I do this/ know this: Y/N	I need further support and guidance in these areas (outline what you feel they are)	Action to be taken and by whom
The NQT is observed within the first four weeks of taking up the post			
All observations have an agreed focus. Written/oral feedback is constructive and prompt			
Termly action plans are reviewed regularly against the standards to ensure good progress is made			
Termly assessments are carried out formally and NQTs know well in advance what is expected of them. Any judgements I make are rigorous, fair and based on sound evidence			
Senior leaders and other stakeholders understand the induction programme and know what I am doing			
I consult the NQTs regularly and involve them in the processes of induction			

Figure 3.5 NQT induction tutor checklist – day-to-day procedures

Criteria	Do I/would I meet this Y/N	What action do I need to take?
The induction tutor should model exemplary professional standards in all aspects of their work in the school		
The induction tutor should invest sufficient time in communicating effectively with all of those colleagues who play a part in the induction year, particularly the new member of staff and their chosen mentor		
The induction tutor should ensure that the induction year is tailor made to meet the needs of individuals and not just 'one size fits all'		
The induction tutor should be confident about any systems of monitoring or evaluation of the role of others involved in the induction year, based on the principle of the entitlement of NQTs to an excellent induction into the profession		
The induction tutor should model the best practice principles of CPD as outlined in previous chapters		
The induction tutor should plan the year to ensure that NQTs are increasingly proactively engaged with the induction process		

Figure 3.6   Welcome letter – new staff to the school/organization

Dear new member of staff

I hope that you are enjoying your holiday and having a good rest before the start of the new term! We are looking forward to seeing you again in September.

I am enclosing a booklet which I hope you will find informative. It outlines different aspects of the school which you may wish to look at before you arrive. I enclose an induction programme designed for all new staff which will keep you informed of key school issues and processes as the term progresses.

School will start [with an Inset day] on [day and date] September at [time]. Please go to the staff room at [time] where I shall meet with you before the staff meeting. I have enclosed a copy of the timetable for the day for your information.

Please also find enclosed a copy of your timetable and the name and details of your 'buddy' mentor in school who is very happy for you to contact him/her before school starts should you have any queries or concerns.

If you have any concerns please do not hesitate to contact me at home.

Yours sincerely

CPD co-ordinator

Encs: Inset day schedule
           Timetable for induction of new staff
           Welcome booklet
           Personal timetable
           Buddy mentor details/CPD co-ordinator details

Figure 3.7   Induction timetable for staff new to the school

TIMETABLE FOR INDUCTION OF
NEW STAFF – 200X/200Y

*** Indicates those sessions which both teaching and support staff may find useful**

Day and Date	Topic
E.g. Wednesday 7 September	Introducing the support staff and Senior Resources Manager **
	Getting to know your department/team – an opportunity to familiarize yourself with your departmental/team policies, handbooks, resources, etc.**
	CPD – introduction to the staff development pro formas and current practices **
	Health and Safety issues in the workplace **
	Inset Day – no meeting
	SEN/Inclusion – key issues lead by SENCO **

Half Term

Using performance data/reporting arrangements

Core policies and procedures including behaviour management **

The role of the governing body **

CPD co-ordinator available in staff room for individual queries **

Nearly there – come and celebrate making it through the first term with a mince pie and a glass of wine! All staff invited! Staff Room

All meetings will be held in [state venue] unless otherwise informed nearer the date – from 3.10 to approximately 3.45.

Figure 3.8   Memo to buddy mentors

MEMO FROM: CPD co-ordinator
TO: All buddy mentors of new staff
DATE:

Dear

Many thanks once again for volunteering to buddy mentor a new member of staff. With X number of new staff this year, there will be lots of new faces and your support will be invaluable in helping new colleagues to settle in quickly and effectively.

I will put a list of all new staff and their mentors on the notice board in September – your mentee will be .... in the .... department. A letter will now go out to all new staff with the names of their buddy mentors and information they will need before September. I will also put together a programme of induction after school on [day] to which all new staff are invited to attend – venue to be confirmed and which you may wish to remind them of – I'll put a copy also on the notice board.

Your role is primarily to help staff settle in during the first few days perhaps in the following ways:

- Approach him/her at the beginning and end of the first few days if you can and ask how he/she is getting on.
- Invite him/her to have coffee in the staffroom. Please be proactive – new staff may be nervous about approaching <u>you</u>!
- Make a point of having lunch with him/her in the first few days and from time to time throughout the year – this should be easier to arrange with the e-mail system.
- Catch up with him/her at intervals throughout the year to offer advice/support if needed.
- Send him/her a Xmas card!

In the case of NQTs:

- As well as the above it would be wonderful if you could set up a more structured arrangement, i.e. make a point of seeing him/her on a more regular basis and keep this going through the year.

PLEASE DO NOT UNDERESTIMATE HOW MUCH VALUE IS PLACED ON HAVING A FRIENDLY FACE OUTSIDE THE DEPARTMENT/FACULTY. PLEASE ACTIVELY SEEK OUT NEW COLLEAGUES FROM TIME TO TIME – WHEN THE SYSTEM WORKS, NEW COLLEAGUES DERIVE ENORMOUS BENEFIT FROM YOUR SUPPORT AND GUIDANCE AND THIS IS VALUABLE, INFORMAL AND ONGOING CPD.

Please let me know immediately if you feel a new member of staff is finding it difficult or has a concern. This will then be dealt with by HODs/team leaders or myself. Don't hesitate to ask me if you have any questions. Once again many thanks.

Key aspects of the induction year for NQTs

Supporting the mentor in establishments where this is not the induction tutor

In many secondary schools the induction tutor will not be the mentor working closely with the NQT. If this is the case in your school, then you will need to invest considerable time and effort in making sure that those subject leaders/other mentors chosen are completely clear about their responsibilities, understand the induction standards and the statutory nature of the year and are comfortable about the procedures and systems you have put in place to ensure the year goes well. The meeting agenda in Figure 3.9 covers the key aspects of what those who are working closely with NQTs need to know. This meeting can be led by you or might provide a good CPD opportunity for mentors who have previously worked with NQTs and 'know the ropes'.

The overview schema of the year might look something like that in Figure 3.10.

At this stage you will want to keep things as simple as possible while ensuring that everyone involved feels confident about their role and the timings of key aspects of the year.

Action planning against the standards

The key to an effective induction year is continuity at all stages throughout to ensure that good progress is made against the standards. Most newly qualified staff will leave their further education establishment with a Career Entry and Development Profile which induction tutors should use to ensure that we are as informed as possible about the strengths and areas for development of the NQT in question. The areas for development identified can then be discussed and form the basis of the first action plan (Figure 3.11).

Subsequent termly action plans should take forward the areas for development which have been identified by those involved with the NQT as evidenced through observation, meetings, and so on, and which were discussed with the NQT during the assessment meeting and recorded on the Induct 1 assessment forms for terms 1 and 2. All those who are involved with supporting the NQT should have the opportunity to provide feedback on progress judged against the standards; it is then the induction tutor's job to collate these into detailed statements, which of course should be evidenced. Encourage NQTs to keep clearly signposted evidence against each of the induction standards, which can then be referenced to their ongoing professional portfolio.

Action plan objectives should be shared with the mentor and other colleagues where they will be supporting the NQT in some way, and should be regularly reviewed to make sure that the NQT is on track to meet them.

As I have mentioned before, it is my opinion that we have a duty to NQTs to model excellence in our own professional practices when working with them. It is for this reason that I always have a typed agenda for any meeting. This need not be onerous or time-consuming. I have included in this section an agenda for a typical formal assessment meeting (Figure 3.12) which you can adapt and which will save you time and energy. Before the meeting takes place – ensure that NQTs are fully informed of what the purpose of the meeting is and what they will need to bring (Figure 3.13) Given that they will possibly be anxious about the meeting, it is really important that the induction tutor keeps communication as open and supportive as possible.

**Figure 3.9   CPD Meeting with HODs/other professional
mentor – agenda exemplar**

INDUCTION OF NQTs

Date:

Present:

Agenda

- General outline of induction procedures – copy of induction standards and how to use them

- Overview schema of year issued

- Agreement of timetable of observations in autumn term along with follow-up discussion and feedback

- Discussion of LEA support programme for NQTs, local networking groups and the school-based induction programme for all new staff

- Opportunities for professional development within school and clarification of the use of 10% remission time

- Regular support meetings; the nature and use of these

- Use of Career Entry and Development Profile (CEDP)

- Coaching partnerships in school available for new mentors

- Questions

Figure 3.10   Overview schema of NQT induction year arrangements

Term 1

Meet with Induction Tutor to agree first term action plan and to set objectives for induction based on CEDP, school context and the Induction Standards

- Observation to be carried out by IT and HOD/other professional mentor
- IT and HOD to agree observation outcomes
- IT to feed back, review progress and objectives

Half Term

- Observation of NQT by HOD/other professional mentor and follow-up discussion
- Meeting with HOD to review progress

Assessment meeting 1 with Induction Tutor
Focus of meeting – consistency in continuing to meet standards for QTS and Induction Standards
Report sent by HT

Term 2

- Action plan for second term of teaching drawn up. Based on agreed areas for development from first term as outlined on Induct 1 form
- Observation of NQT by HOD and follow-up discussion
- Meeting to review progress and objectives

Half Term

- Observation of NQT by IT
- Meeting to review progress and objectives

Assessment meeting 2 with Induction Tutor
Focus of meeting – progress in meeting Induction Standards
Report sent by HT

Term 3

- Observation of NQT by HOD and follow-up discussion
- Meeting to review progress and objectives

Half Term

- Observation of NQT by County Adviser in subject or other appropriate external professional
- Meeting with IT to review progress and consider objectives for second year of teaching

---

Assessment meeting 3 with Induction Tutor
Focus of meeting – whether the NQT has met the Induction Standards
IT and NQT agree professional objectives for year 2 based on the outcomes of the year's progress
These are recorded on staff development pro forma

The headteacher sends recommendations to the appropriate body which then makes a final decision and informs NQT, DfES, GTC and NQT's employer

Photocopiable: The CPD Co-ordinator's Toolkit
Paul Chapman Publishing 2006 © Sue Kelly

Figure 3.11 Example objectives and action plan for first term of first year of teaching

Name:

Objectives	Induction Standard reference	Actions to be taken and by whom	Success criteria	Resources	Target date for achievement	Review date
• To assess developmental needs through observation		• One observation by IT • One observation by mentor • Possible informal observation and oral feedback from mentor with a specific focus	• That appropriate targets for development are set and supported by the professional tutor and the Head of Department	• Possible need for protected frees for periods of observation	• Specify date for each objective identified	• Specify date for each objective identified
• To focus on differentiation in planning and materials in line with the Induction Standards, particularly in relation to the least able		• NQT to research recent developments in pedagogy in this area and to collate ideas from other members of the dept. • IT to organize input from SENCO. • Mentor/IT to make this an observation focus and provide feedback	• There will be clear evidence of differentiation in lesson planning and materials in relation to this target	• Expertise of SENCO • Meeting time for NQTs to share learning outcomes. • Possible need for protected frees for periods of observation		
• To incorporate more collaborative group and pair work into planning		• To develop classroom practice through working with the Pedagogy and Practice materials and keeping a learning journal of learning outcomes and successful practice	• That planning incorporates clearly these elements and this is observed in teaching as evidenced in observations by mentor and IT	• Resources available from IT • Use of remission time for working with Pedagogy and Practice materials.		
Signature on behalf of employer:			Date:	Signature of NQT:		Date:

Figure 3.12   NQT assessment meeting agenda

Date:

Time:

Venue:

Present: NQT and IT (give names)

- Outline of meeting and clarification of purpose

- Review of current action plan

- Induction Standards assessment against the following headings:

    - Teaching

    - Professional values and practices

    - Knowledge and understanding

Please bring supportive documentation to the meeting, for example your ongoing professional portfolio signposted against the Induction Standard headings.

- Discussion and completion of statements under headings on assessment report form

- Remission time – documentation and discussion of use of. Review of all ongoing CPD and impact

- Agreement of professional objectives against the Induction Standards for inclusion on next term's action plan

- Other issues

Figure 3.13   Example memo to NQTs pre-assessment meeting

MESSAGE FROM: Induction tutor	TO: NQTs

DATE:

Dear

I will be holding your assessment meeting to finalize the documentation for the completion of your first/second term of induction on [date and time]. I will request cover for you/protect your non-contact period [whichever applies].

Please could you bring the following along with you as part of the supporting evidence:

- Your teacher planner/other types of lesson plans

- Record of your use of 10% remission time

- Your ongoing professional portfolio

- Any other records/evidence you think may be useful such as self-assessment, lesson evaluations or examples of pupils' work/pupil feedback/ongoing assessment records/register of groups, etc.

I have a copy of all observations/meetings with HODS/your mentor so we should have plenty of supporting evidence to back up the statements. The objective of the meeting is to assess your progress against the Induction Standards, to affirm strengths and to identify areas for further development. This form will then be sent to County as confirmation of you having successfully completed the first/second term of your Induction year.

The meeting will be held in my office [say where this is!] and will probably take between 45 minutes to an hour.

Best wishes

[Induction tutor name]

I have always requested that NQTs provide me with a brief summary of what was discussed at the assessment meeting for three main reasons:

1. It gives me a clear picture of how well NQTs are understanding the processes involved in the induction year, including the purpose of the assessment meeting itself.

2. I feel it is important to engage NQTs fully and proactively in these processes as important modelling for their future professional lives.

3. The summary or action points from the meeting need to be clearly recorded for inclusion on the next action plan to be distributed to all those involved in helping the NQTs to meet the objectives agreed.

Ongoing CPD

All newly qualified staff are entitled to a 10% reduction to their normal timetable which should be used for ongoing professional development activities and which should be identified as such on their timetables. As induction tutor/CPD co-ordinator it is fundamental that we are fully committed and confident about the importance of the following as valuable CPD activities which can be recorded on the remission time log kept by NQTs:

✓ regular meeting slots with an experienced subject mentor

✓ the opportunity to be observed regularly and to receive well-focused and constructive critiques of their work to ensure that good progress is made

✓ the opportunity to observe other colleagues within and outside of an NQT's own department/faculty/team/school

✓ the value of time spent reflecting on the above with learning outcomes recorded in an ongoing professional journal, which can form the basis of discussion with the mentor or induction tutor.

It is also important that induction tutors facilitate the following experiences for newly qualified staff:

✓ a visit to another school(s) with a focus on an area identified from the action plan against the induction standards

✓ the opportunity to network with other NQTs from other schools

✓ the opportunity to meet regularly with the induction tutor to review progress against the action plan targets

✓ the opportunity to meet as an NQT group with the onus on NQTs driving the agenda to ensure that the planned programme of meetings meets their needs not those of the induction tutor

✓ the opportunity to engage in and to value the myriad CPD activities which occur informally on a day-to-day basis or through more formal arrangements as outlined on the individual staff development pro forma and which now should be reflected in the culture of learning in your school/institution.

Top tips for induction tutors

✓ Be rigorous, encouraging and challenging in a way which will get the best out of newly qualified staff and at the same time make explicit for them the highest professional standards.

✓ Make sure you fully involve and engage NQTs during the year: ask them to record the outcomes of assessment meetings as a way of ensuring that they understand the processes and rationale of the year; ask them to set the agenda for group meetings which you can then facilitate.

✓ Ask NQTs to keep a learning journal – this does not have to be time-consuming but should record and crystallize the key learning outcomes of every CPD activity in which they are engaged; what a powerful and useful document this will then become as a point of referral in future years.

✓ If possible, arrange for an external observer to observe one of their lessons before the final term's assessment, in order to ensure that each NQT has objective feedback on his/her strengths and areas for development at the end of the year; these will translate into powerful professional objectives for their second year of teaching.

✓ Encourage NQTs to give a presentation on a recent development in their subject/area of pedagogy; not only is this a great CPD opportunity in itself for them and for colleagues who will see the presentation, but it is also a way of highlighting the need to keep abreast of current developments in their subject/teaching and learning in general which is so fundamental to the requirements of the National Standards. They can also use this as evidence for that section of the standards!

Points to remember:

- Model the highest professional standards through your own practices at all times – this is the best CPD you can organize for newly qualified colleagues!
- Develop sound communication channels if you are not the subject mentor for NQTs. Keeping everyone in the loop is fundamental to continuity and consistency for NQTs in their induction year.
- Invest time in ensuring that all of those involved in the induction process are well informed about the requirements and what is involved – and that includes you!
- Be rigorous, fair and consistent in your approach. Work to the principles of entitlement and be confident about the importance of this.

Teachernet has a useful site for newly qualified teachers, induction tutors and CPD co-ordinators. Go to www.teachernet.gov.uk/professionaldevelopment/for more information.

CPD for support staff

The School Workforce and Development Board (SWDB) is chaired by the Teacher Development Agency (TDA) and charged with guiding the TDA's work on the training and development of school support staff. For most of us working as CPD co-ordinators in schools, the issue of providing a coherent CPD programme to meet the needs of an ever-increasing and complex range of support staff roles is likely to be an area of our work where we feel dissatisfied with our performance or confused as to what our input should be.

The three priorities which have been identified by the SDWB for action in the near future are to:

✓ improve the provision of development training for support staff

✓ ensure that all development and training activities are of a high quality

✓ break down any barriers in the workplace which prevent support staff being involved in or taking up training and development opportunities.

The role of the CPD co-ordinator

In previous chapters I have made reference to the ways in which all staff can be included in the provision for and planning of CPD activities which meet their needs in the school. With the impact of the workforce reform agenda being felt in schools and educational institutions across the country 'there is an increasing emphasis on building the whole school team – leadership, teachers, and support staff – so that, working together, everyone can make a more powerful contribution to the overall objective of raising standards' (Stephen Twigg's Foreword to *Building the School Team* compiled by the SWDB).

When considering the needs of this key group of staff, our role as facilitator and co-ordinator of all CPD practices in the school is to ensure that:

✓ the systems and practices in place are inclusive of support staff wherever possible

✓ the key principles of good practice CPD are applied across the whole staff where these are appropriate (see beginning of this chapter for an overview of best practice principles)

✓ we consult with the line managers or team leaders of individuals/groups of support staff to develop the school CPD systems and procedures with the needs of the whole staff in mind

✓ team leaders/line managers of support staff are clear about the need to establish clear competencies and job descriptions for the various categories of support staff which either directly or indirectly support the School Improvement Plan. In this way identification of CPD needs at support staff review or appraisal meetings can be recorded on the support staff individual development pro forma and planned provision can be made

✓ we encourage deployment of expertise across the whole staff for the benefit of individual and team CPD

✓ we challenge old-fashioned attitudes and begin to recognize that the body of support staff working in schools has much to contribute to the CPD of teaching staff. Information and communication support staff or skilled administrators can play a key role in developing the ICT skills of teaching staff; highly trained laboratory assistants can be deployed to work with teaching colleagues, training them in new techniques; maintenance staff may be qualified to run health and safety courses for others, for example, working at height and ladder training; Learning Support Assistants can provide valuable feedback to teaching staff which may inform future CPD needs; catering managers may support the knowledge and understanding of those who are moving forward the government's Healthy Schools agenda

✓ we be creative in the way we team up individual or groups of teaching and support staff to capitalize on the expertise which teaching colleagues can draw on to induct support staff and develop their behaviour management, for example, assertive discipline skills

✓ we have an overview of team planning in order to co-ordinate and amalgamate training input, with an emphasis on good value.

With a bit of creative thinking we can play an instrumental role in pulling together the whole of the staff to create a dynamic learning community; one where each individual is committed to his/her own learning and that of others. In the business of learning, what better way to inspire and motivate the whole staff than by making sure that everyone understands the importance of their role in impacting on students' learning in classrooms. What an exciting and uniting thought!

For further information on the subject of support staff CPD, the TDA website provides a useful starting point. Go to http://www.tda.gov.uk/support.aspx.

You may find useful the Teachers TV programme, *Secondary CPD in Action: Personalising CPD*. Go to www.teachers.tv. Select "video library", then "secondary" and "headteacher/senior manager" options.

CHAPTER 4

Embedding good practice

This chapter will provide you with both formal and informal ways of embedding your good practice CPD approaches to date. From conversations you may have with individual staff or team leaders through to the production of a clear guidance booklet, the communication of a clear vision for CPD practices will reinforce key messages for staff. Gauge where you are in leading CPD practices at whole-school level if you are in a small school or institution, or how far middle leaders have moved forward in larger schools, by issuing a straightforward questionnaire which will inform your practice and enable you to deploy still further the expertise available at this/these levels. A fascinating case study focuses on developing and embedding coaching and action research models in an Early Professional Development programme at Littlehampton Community School; a progressive approach which builds on good practice induction for NQTs as outlined in the previous chapter and which can easily be adapted to meet a variety of CPD needs across the entire staff.

Informal approaches

You should by now have begun to feel the buzz of learning vibrating through your school or institution. Your job from now on involves talking up CPD and celebrating wherever it is happening. You have already supported staff to recognize the value of learning from each other and to recognize not only the expertise which they can tap into from others, but also to recognize their own strengths which can be exploited for the good of other colleagues. Using the staff development pro forma will have resulted in more focused and strategic use of resources and your middle/team leaders will be beginning to lead CPD for their own teams in more creative and imaginative ways. Your vision is clear and it would be easy to think your job is done – but it is crucial that you guard against complacency. There are many things which you can do to help embed these good practices, and so many require just a bit of thoughtfulness on your part which really can make all the difference.

Some of your work involves taking the simplest of actions:

✓ Recognize CPD where it is happening and point it out. When a colleague is demonstrating a simple operation to enhance the use of ICT to another in the staffroom you can proffer 'Great CPD!' When strategies to handle the difficult behaviour of a student form the basis of discussion in a meeting, just an acknowledgement of the learning involved to support our practices in future keeps CPD on the agenda. You will soon find that other staff follow your lead. In my school it was not long before I was greeted with shouts of, 'Sue – I've just been CPD'd!' It was at those times that I felt the shift of culture best and that was tremendously rewarding.

✓ Seek out those individuals or teams who are taking incremental steps to move forward in their CPD practices and recognize their achievements. 'I saw CPD on your meeting agenda – how did it go?' This can make all the difference to middle/team leaders who are implementing your suggestions and beginning to consider the role they have in leading CPD practices for their own teams.

✓ Take the time to support and show encouragement when invited to see the work of other colleagues who will often be keen to show you what they are doing. I remember just how excited I felt the first time I was invited along to a Modern Foreign Languages department sharing of good practice meeting, 'to see what we're doing'. This investment of your time – no matter how busy you are – will pay dividends.

✓ Offer to spend time chatting through ideas with individual middle leaders who are having difficulty adapting to your new approaches. I sat down with a very experienced head of department who had asked for some help with his CPD planning for the department based on the staff development pro formas. I admit to being not a little surprised when he confessed that he was finding the whole shift of culture extremely challenging as it was forcing him to completely adjust the mindset to staff training and courses that he had developed over years in the profession. Do not underestimate what a threat these new approaches might still be to some staff, who will need plenty of support from you.

Open communication

As a way of consolidating the work done by you and your colleagues so far, it would seem sensible to condense key areas of development of CPD practices into a guidance booklet which staff can consult. The overall content and nature of the booklet can be left entirely to you to fit into your own school or institution's context, but there is no reason why you cannot include articles of pedagogical interest to suit all staff or case studies of good practice, and so on. The fun bit for you, which will also benefit your own professional development, will be to keep abreast of relevant periodicals or other literature as well as using the wealth of material available on the Internet.

No doubt you will have a limited budget for staff development which you will be keen to spend wisely. Cost-effective approaches will now be high on everyone's agenda but the funding you have available is a bonus and should be allocated fairly and openly. In a school or institution with a smaller number of staff it may well be the co-ordinator's job to manage the overall budget; in a larger organization such as a secondary school, like the one in which I work, funds should be allocated to middle leaders to manage with some guidance from you.

The following pages are taken from a guidance booklet for staff which you can adapt with the aim of keeping everyone informed about the nature of CPD practices in the school plus the rationale behind them and the key issues which underpin them. I will assume that, should you find some of these pages useful, you will want to reproduce them in your own school's style and format with an attractive front cover. Rather than reproduce every page of the booklet, which it is unlikely would be relevant to the range of contexts in which we are all working, I have included the contents page as an overview and to give you an idea of how you might want the booklet to look; the rest I'll leave up to you but you may find what follows a useful example of the kinds of information and guidance you wish to share with staff.

Begin by designing your own front cover in the style common to all your school or institution's stationery.

Your contents' page could look something like this:

Figure 4.A   Continuing Professional Development (CPD) Contents

Colour reference to contents	Page 1
Departmental/team budgets	Page 2
CPD at whole-school level	Page 3
Inset days	Page 4
CPD – Managing the process at Any School	Pages 5–6
Cycle of CPD performance review	Page 7
CPD planner 200X/200Y	Page 8
Inset programme and cancellations	Pages 9–10
Any School CPD policy	Pages 11–13
Media articles about CPD	Pages 14–18
Discover CPD in museums	Pages 19–20
Professional centres – how to get there	Pages 21–22
Appendix One	Page 23–24
Staff development pro forma	

Your next page could include:

Figure 4.B   Colour reference to contents

This booklet contains information on the following:

1. Budget share for CPD and departmental allocation (cream)

2. Performance Review and CPD: work in progress (pale blue)

3. CPD: support/ideas for the continued development and impact of this at departmental and pastoral level (pink)

The following are key elements of our CPD practice:

● Targeting funding at *specific, identified* needs

● Value for money and cost-effective approaches

● Monitoring the impact on classroom practice

Be open and transparent about the way any funding is allocated and to whom (Figure 4.1). Any other additional funds can be outlined here and links made where possible to the School Improvement Plan.

You may now wish to outline clearly any other points regarding the systems in place for established CPD practices in school (Figure 4.2).

Figure 4.1 Budget allocation 200X/200Y

A budget total of £   has been allocated for all training across the school. This has been allocated in the following way.

Department	Allocation
English	£
Drama	£
Mathematics	£
Science	£
DT	£
Art	£
Humanities	£
RE	£
MFL	£
PE/Dance	£
Music	£
ICT/Business Studies	£
PSHE	£
SEN	£
Whole-school management Including: Use of Advisers Governors Training SIMS Training SLG Leadership for subject and pastoral leaders Examinations Officer Discretionary	£
Whole-school Inset days	£
Support staff Including: First Aid Technicians Special Training Administration Health and Safety Learning Support	£

Departmental allocation has been based on the number of full and part time staff. Provision has also been made for middle leaders for leadership training to be authorized by [CPD co-ordinator's name]. This is within the whole-school management pot and consists of £   which can cover the cost of an external conference, network meeting, collaborative activity, seminar, etc. or other leadership activities.

Additional Funds:

• National strategy funding

Note: There is an allocation for middle leaders calculated at departmental level which is not the case for SLG members.

Figure 4.2 Points to consider – CPD at whole-school level

Individual staff CPD pro formas have been updated to support current CPD practices and to dovetail these more securely with the performance review procedures in place. These will need to be completed by staff and will form the basis of planning for the leadership and management of CPD at departmental level on the pro forma attached here.

A reminder that many strands feed into the management of CPD at department/team level. There is growing evidence of examples of good practice which can be shared by middle or team leaders.

- The information outlined in departmental/team training requests provides a good starting point for identifying generic needs and targeting funding at these.

- Information from departmental/team observations can be used to match training to the 'Points for Development' of individuals within the department.

- Performance Review targets may be partly based on the above and should form the basis for individual focused CPD in order to support department/team members to achieve them.

- The departmental/team CPD training day can be used in a variety of ways to meet individual and generic training needs.

- Training should also take into account whole school and departmental/team priorities.

- Wherever possible any training activity should be recorded and held in departmental/team records or should encourage the collection of evidence for Professional Development Portfolios, to enable staff to keep a record for future reference. These may then provide useful evidence to support threshold applications etc. The evidence may be a departmental/team agenda, a training resource produced by you, the evaluation of an external visit with a specific focus, for example, and any evidence agreed in advance on the appropriate pro forma regarding the different levels of impact of a CPD activity.

- Budget allocation can be used to fund supply cover for departmental/team CPD in the form of observation of lessons by other colleagues, external visits, e.g. to other schools, planned departmental training by an external provider, etc. but this should be grouped wherever possible to facilitate the cover arrangements involved when bringing in external supply cover staff.

- In order to ensure value for money, the type and quality of feedback **should be planned before a development activity takes place** in order to ensure the dissemination of relevant information across the department and to provide a training opportunity by doing so. This should be recorded on the **Evaluation of the Impact of Planned CPD Activities pro forma** to be completed by all staff prior to agreed CPD activities.

- Spreading professional development opportunities fairly across departmental/team members needs to be taken into account also.

Forward planning using the generic outcomes from the staff development pro formas plus objectives taken from your School Improvement Plan, should put you in a strong position to be able to outline well in advance an overview of the nature and content of Inset days for the forthcoming year. Do this with dates clearly stated and list the whole-school priorities for the year (Figure 4.3). This will then inform the planning of other leaders in the school towards meeting whole-school objectives through CPD activities at a variety of levels. Colleagues may also find it useful to have a clear idea of the cost of external county Inset, plus supply or cover costs needed to cover for colleagues who are out of school on a CPD activity.

The next pages of your guidance booklet should state clearly and explicitly the rationale behind the use of the individual staff development pro forma. It should also serve as a memory jogger for staff to remind them of the key principles of best practice CPD in terms of how it relates to them. You may wish to adapt the pages which follow (Figure 4.4).

The pages reproduced here can be found on the accompanying CD-ROM with the addition of an Any School CPD policy and a possible review cycle with suggested timings for the elements of this process to take place (although this depends very much on your own school calendar), which should provide a basis for you to consider producing or amending your own policy, depending on your context. All you now have to do is to complete the document with additional sections as you wish. For example you may wish to reproduce the staff development pro forma or the department/team planner. You may also wish to include CPD articles of interest such as those mentioned here which are not included but will hopefully give you some ideas. Additionally, you may find it useful to establish a time cycle for the processes outlined in the documentation to ensure that the CPD processes you wish to establish dovetail neatly with your school/institution's performance review processes.

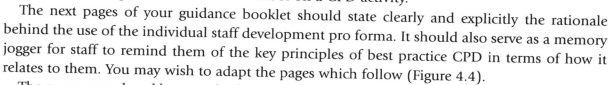

Points to remember

- Invest time in recognizing and celebrating CPD happening on a daily basis in your school/institution.
- Produce a guidance booklet with key CPD information which can be consulted readily by staff and easily updated year on year.
- Be transparent and fair in the way funds are managed.
- In a smaller school or institution, the CPD co-ordinator may be responsible for leading and managing CPD with a more 'hands on' approach. Use the guidance above and substitute CPD co-ordinator for middle leader where appropriate.
- Keep the School Improvement Plan at the heart of all CPD practices.

Distributed leadership – deploying and developing expertise

Having supported middle/team leaders to transform their own CPD practices it is now time to take stock and gauge the level of expertise at this level, which you can deploy to even greater effect. When the time is right and colleagues have had a chance to get to grips with the changing culture and new approaches, use the questionnaire in Figure 4.6 to support you in your role as CPD co-ordinator and facilitator. If you are the co-ordinator in a smaller school/institution then simply use the questions as prompts to further develop your own practices, perhaps in discussion with a member of the senior leadership group. Where the questions refer to a department or faculty, substitute 'staff in your school'.

Figure 4.3   Inset days

There are five Inset days during the academic year 200X/200Y. The dates of these are shown below and are also on the school calendar.

It is envisaged that these days will be based on the following outline agendas:

1.

2.

3.

4.

5.

Whole-school priorities include: [examples are given here]

- Assessment for learning

- Enhancing the quality of teaching by extending the detail of feedback following a lesson observation

- To increase access to ICT through an integrated e-learning strategy including Virtual Learning Environment (VLE)

- Extending collaboration through the LIG group/Interlos/Comenius projects

County courses are run at a cost of £   per day. The cost of supply cover is approximately £   .

Figure 4.4   A guide to the management of CPD for teaching staff

CPD at whole-school level

All staff will be asked to complete and regularly update a staff development pro forma in order to provide the CPD co-ordinator and your head of department/team leader with information about identified targets and ways of matching these to professional development opportunities. This information is collated in order to provide training opportunities as requested wherever possible and to identify whole school training needs. It will form the basis of your Head of Department/team leader's plan for the management of CPD within your department/ area.

The managing of CPD at departmental/faculty level

Middle leaders will consider the following:

- The information outlined in departmental training requests. This will provide a good starting point for identifying generic needs and targeting funding at these.

- Information from departmental observations. This can be used to match training to your 'Points for Development' following an observation.

- Performance Review targets. These may be partly based on the above and should form the basis for focused CPD in order to support you to achieve them.

- How best to use the departmental CPD day, for example this day can be used in a variety of ways to meet individual and generic training needs within your department.

- Wherever possible any training activity should be recorded and held in departmental records or should encourage the collecting of evidence for Professional Development Portfolios, to enable staff to keep a record for future reference. These may then provide useful evidence to support, for example, a threshold application etc. The evidence may be a departmental agenda, a training resource or evaluation of an external visit you carried out with a specific focus to meet an identified objective on your personal pro forma.

- Budget allocation can be used to fund supply cover for departmental CPD. This may be in the form of observation of lessons by other colleagues, external visits to other schools, planned departmental training by an external provider, etc. Time should be blocked wherever possible to facilitate the cover arrangements involved when bringing in external supply cover staff.

- The type and quality of **feedback** of a development activity. **This should be planned before the development activity takes place, where appropriate, in order to ensure the dissemination of relevant information across the department and to provide a training opportunity by doing so.**

- The spreading of professional development opportunities fairly across department/team members.

You may wish to consider the following:

- The range of CPD activities available to you (copy attached of the professional development pro forma).

- The importance of keeping a record of any professional development activity and the evidence for this in a professional portfolio.

- The need to discuss your professional development ideas with your head of department, team leader or line manager in order to target specific areas of your classroom performance or career development.

- The value of internal/external observation of colleagues within (or outside of) your own department with a specific focus.

- How you will monitor/provide evidence that a professional development activity has had an impact on your performance.

- How you will demonstrate that you have been proactive in fulfilling your CPD needs.

- How you would justify a CPD activity in terms of it meeting an identified development need either personal or otherwise.

NOTE: INSERT OTHER DOCUMENTS BETWEEN PAGE 6 AND PAGE 12 AS REQUIRED ACCORDING TO YOUR CONTENTS' PAGE.

Figure 4.5   Example school policy: Continuing Professional Development

Rationale

Staff will be given the opportunity to develop professional knowledge and skills both from a personal point of view and also to keep abreast of new initiatives – nationally, locally and within school.

Aims

1.   To provide ongoing training for staff in order to meet national requirements for all teachers.

2.   To develop and motivate the individual member of staff and provide opportunities for them to broaden their experience whilst fostering a proactive approach to CPD on the part of the individual.

3.   To assist and promote the quality of teaching and learning by developing the professional skills of all the staff, both teaching and support.

4.   To provide value for money through a planned approach and targeted on individual, departmental and whole-school needs.

5.   To promote creative and imaginative approaches to CPD which place value on the expertise in-house and encourage sharing of good practice, and active dissemination of new skills and knowledge.

6.   To create a culture of learning in the school.

Objectives

Staff development must:

- Support the school's aim to strive for quality and excellence and to set high standards for all.

- Provide staff training to allow the annual development plan to be carried out and targets to be met through:

  - the School Improvement Plan – identifies whole school needs
  - team plans which collate individual and team professional targets which will require CPD input.

- Provide staff training to develop individual personnel through close analysis of CPD pro formas and performance management to identify individual needs.

- Offer special provision for the induction of Newly Qualified Staff and new staff.

- Offer provision for existing staff taking on new responsibilities.

- Offer confidential status to personal requests.

- Operate within the constraints of the allocated development budget.

- Set priorities in order to match the needs of the individual with those of the school.

Be evaluated for its effectiveness in:

- Improving and monitoring the quality of teaching, learning and care of the pupils.

- Providing value for money.

- Promoting job satisfaction, personal achievement, individual and team work and personal advancement.

- Raising staff awareness of the school's ethos, philosophy, aims and objectives.

- Developing the individual in ways that will help to improve the effectiveness of the whole school.

- Monitoring the impact of all CPD practices and activities on professional practice in the classroom and the learning of students.

Implementation

Identification of needs:

- Through requests from middle leaders' plans and analysis of performance review.

- Through consultation with departments, HODs, HOYs, SMT, individual staff and the headteacher.

- Through analysis of CPD pro formas and subsequent planning to meet targeted needs at departmental and whole school level.

- By monitoring through the HOD/HOY/team leader; for example, through formal observation procedures which identify areas for development.

School-based training carried out in a range of ways through:

- Use of planned CPD activities in departmental time: either item on CPD meetings agenda or use of Inset time.

- Use of whole-school Inset days.

- Other possibilities – job shadowing, 'buddying', team teaching, job-swaps.

- Planned Inset with an external provider.

- Proactive planned management of CPD at departmental level/year group level in line with the national standards for subject leaders.

Off-site training and development:

- Courses (LEA, external providers).

- Courses (national).

- International professional development – Comenius.

▶

- Visits to other schools.

- Common Inset days and networking opportunities to meet other teachers to discuss a common theme.

Review

- Evaluation every time provision has been made.

- Through discussion in SMT/SCDC/within departments.

- Through meetings with the SMT/school's resources manager.

- An annual evaluation to provide an overview and way forward – report to the HT.

Resources

- Time for consultation with staff.

- Training support for HODs/HOYs to manage CPD at departmental level.

Reporting

- To the governors annually.

- To the HT each term.

- To the resources manager to keep up to date with the accounts.

Photocopiable: The CPD Co-ordinator's Toolkit
Paul Chapman Publishing 2006 © Sue Kelly

By collating the feedback from the completed questionnaires you should have some powerful information to take your own work forward and to develop the skills and expertise of middle leaders still further. The information you have gleaned will provide you with a quick and efficient tool for gauging the strengths and areas of expertise of those key personnel working at this middle leaders level. In a smaller context – you should have identified for yourself where your practice is strong and where you need support. You are now in a position to consult your SLG with some focused objectives to develop your own professional competency. Alternatively, in a large institution, you can now use this invaluable feedback, in the style of effective CPD practices, to disseminate and share good practice, to utilize expertise and to support weaker practice wherever it exists. Consider the following approaches:

Figure 4.6   Middle leaders' questionnaire to support CPD practices

In order to support you with the above could you please answer the following questions in detail:

1. Would you be able to provide a member of your department/colleague, on request, with an up-to-date record of any course, external Inset, network meeting or external collaboration which they have attended or participated in during the last two years? If so, how and where is this information kept?
   ....
   ....

2. Would you feel able to provide your SLG with:

   a. An up-to-date record of the professional development opportunities you have provided for members of your department/team and how this information is kept?
   ....
   ....
   ....

   b. An indication of how these opportunities match the CPD requests on individual pink staff pro formas which staff completed and which were copied to you last year?
   ....
   ....
   ....

   c. An indication of how the planned professional development activity you provided matched a development need identified from lesson observation, performance review targets, departmental targets or whole-school targets?
   ....
   ....
   ....

3. Would you feel able to provide, on request, an outline of the specific ICT training needs of your department and how you plan to provide for these/are leading these? Please detail below.
   ....
   ....
   ....

4. How well do you know your department/team?

   a. Could you identify individuals in your department with a particular level of expertise, e.g. advanced ICT skills, consistent and continued success with low ability groups/ number of grade A* passes at GCSE, etc. How is this information kept?
   ....
   ....

   b. Could you provide evidence that use of the above expertise forms part of your planning for your leadership and management of staff development? Please detail below how this works.
   ....
   ....
   ....

▶

c. Do you include CPD as an item on the agenda of department/team meetings?
If so what aspects have you covered since September? Please briefly outline how your CPD input has matched individual, departmental or whole-school identified training needs.

....

....

....

6. Professional development and support for middle leaders in the last 18 months has included the following: [adapt the following list to your own context]

- Inset time dedicated to identifying staff CPD requests and ideas for managing these at department level.

- The use and development of a professional portfolio.

- Performance Review Conference for HODs and seconds in department.

- Observation techniques.

- Support for planning for – pupils achieving marginally
                                          – behaviour management.

- Information booklet on budget allocation, county Inset, staff development, and ideas for managing this cost-effectively at departmental/team level.

Given the above, what further professional development do you feel that *you* need in order to be able to continue to effectively manage and support the continuing professional development of each member of your department/team?

....

....

....

6. How do you monitor/how could you begin to monitor more closely the impact of any CPD activity on classroom practice? (This is an Ofsted-identified national area of weakness in CPD practices.)

....

....

....

7. Please outline below any CPD activities which you feel have been particularly successful in addressing individual, departmental or whole-school needs which could be shared with other HODS/colleagues as an example(s) of good practice.

....

....

....

✓ Share exemplary practice at every opportunity. This may be in the form of a presentation in a slot for middle leaders on an Inset day or at a middle leaders' group meeting. Ask for feedback from the recipients on how their own practices have changed as a result. Share this also. Do not underestimate what a great CPD opportunity this is for the person(s) presenting; the opportunity to showcase areas of their work should be motivating for them too, plus it will inspire others.

✓ Set up coaching partnerships which mutually benefit the participants. Ask for a copy of a coaching agreement which clearly outlines what each person involved would like to gain from the coaching, what the success criteria would be and a date for completion if appropriate. Evaluate the impact on future work.

✓ Where weaker practice is in evidence, suggest that this be included as part of the objectives for future performance review targets. You can then support individuals, perhaps through creating an individual action plan, to develop practices in a particular area of their work with CPD.

Points to remember

- It is worth reviewing the work of middle/team leaders in order to establish where there are pockets of good practice which you can share.
- Adapt the questionnaire to suit the needs of those who are leading specific teams of support staff.
- Where there are weaknesses in practice, support individuals to move forward by setting up coaching or mentoring partnerships.

Coaching and mentoring programmes to support ongoing professional development

Both coaching and mentoring 'are effective means of supporting the professional development of teachers in the workplace. They can encourage the development of professional learning and can provide a cost effective method of supporting CPD' (DfES, 2005: 21).

Many schools across the country are using coaching and mentoring to develop the skills of individuals and groups of individuals across the school. However, it is important to understand the differences between the role of mentor and coach. I have reproduced here an excerpt from the DfES guidance booklet referred to above which many co-ordinators will find useful when considering how best to meet the needs of staff and which will provide a useful starting point for those co-ordinators wishing to engage staff to participate in supporting the CPD of others in this way.

Effective approaches

Mentoring and coaching both lead to the establishment of systems that connect specialist support with day-to-day practice and sustained learning over time.

- Mentoring is usually the support of teachers whilst they make a significant career transition. It concerns professional identity in the round and encompasses all aspects of the role. Mentoring is most common in the support of initial teacher training and education, in the support of induction for newly qualified teachers (NQTs) and in supporting teachers moving into leadership roles. Mentoring might well include coaching but will extend beyond it.
- Coaching is concerned with focusing deeply on developing a specific aspect of practice. It may be provided by specialists or peers, and can occur right across the system in a range of forms and contexts. It is particularly useful in building upon and extending, specialist external inputs in day-to-day practice. It is a structured and supportive form of on-the-job support. It can be instrumental in developing a positive climate for adult learning across the school as a whole.
- Many teachers find these approaches attractive, and the reality of support from a mentor or coach challenging, supportive and sustainable. Such approaches, therefore, have the potential to increase a school's capacity for supporting professional learning.

Mentors should:

- **develop** a broad and explicit learning agreement with the person they are mentoring. This will encompass a range of topics. Processes may extend from factual briefing about basic information, through shared planning linked to observation to, at the other extreme, providing access to personal counselling
- **draw** upon the wide range of skills, expertise and opportunities available locally and broker access to such resources
- **use** formative assessment to support progress towards goals and set clear expectations of both partners
- **underpin** progress towards self directed learning through planned, staged and agreed withdrawal of guidance and support as professional skills and confidence grow
- **make** sure that learning programmes and activities take account of the need for trust to enable professional learners to take risks
- **generate** an atmosphere of trust, boundary setting, particularly in relation to assessment or accreditation, and confidentiality
- **make** sure there are opportunities to learn from observing the practice of others, as well as being observed, receiving feedback and reflecting on evidence
- **contribute** to a mentoring culture that recognizes the learning benefits for mentors as well as those being mentored and builds upon these strategically
- **recognise** that mentoring requires skill and experience and make sure that mentors have access to professional development opportunities both as they become mentors and as they enhance their practice on a continuing basis; consider 'mentoring and coaching' for mentors.

Coaches should:

- **establish** learning agreements between coaches and those whom they coach. These should make clear each person's expectations, and set boundaries for the relationships and the confidentiality of the information being shared
- **start** with developing shared understanding of learning goals that are largely framed by the person who is being coached
- **develop** coaching cycles which include shared planning for integrating new approaches into practice, learning from observation, shared interpretation of experimental, practice and/or development experiences and joint reflection on next steps
- **take turns** in peer coaching, to support each other. The commitment to reciprocal learning helps to establish the trust needed for risk taking. It also makes explicit the significant learning benefits inherent in both roles.

(DfES, 2005: 22. © Crown copyright 2005, DfES 0188-2005G.)

There are many opportunities to engage external specialist support in setting up coaching models to support CPD practices. This type of model would also support the needs of governors and the school leadership team, as would participation in the many online discussion forums where the ideas of other colleagues far and wide can be engaged to support work done in school.

CASE STUDY

Littlehampton Community School (LCS) – Coaching and early professional development

Shaun Allison explains how coaching and action research models support the professional development of EPD teachers at his school.

When I took up my role of Assistant Head (Staff Development), I set myself three areas that I wanted to develop at the school:

- coaching
- action research
- early professional development of teachers.

LCS is recognized locally as a school that shows very good practice when it comes to Initial Teacher Training (ITT) and NQT mentoring. It was therefore not surprising, that the responses from a CPD questionnaire that I issued to staff, showed a perception that 'mentoring/coaching with feedback on performance' as a CPD activity was used very well. However, this probably highlighted a misconception concerning the differences between mentoring and coaching. There was little evidence to suggest that 'peer coaching' was taking place, in any kind of structured way. This was seen by myself and the Deputy Head (Teaching and Learning), Steve Nelmes, as a good place to start.

We gave ourselves the task of identifying LCS staff who we thought had shown the potential to be good coaches. The criteria we used to identify our coaches were:

- good classroom practitioners
- good listeners
- positive outlook
- reflective
- professional.

We came up with a list of 13. We could have picked many more, but we wanted to keep this initial group small and manageable. They came from a complete cross-section of the staff – ranging from those who were just about to complete their NQT year, through to Heads of Department – and everything in between! These colleagues were approached and asked if they would be interested in taking part in the programme. They all agreed, except one.

▶

The next step was to give them some training in the skills of coaching. We were very aware that there were many people who were claiming to be 'experts in coaching' but, in reality, very few people who have had a proven track record of success with it. In my previous school, which was in special measures, I had been fortunate enough to work alongside the independent consultant, Michael Harbour. Michael has been a driving force behind setting up coaching programmes in schools across the country – with a great deal of success. Michael came into school for two days in early May 2005, to train our group of prospective coaches. This was an intensive, but highly rewarding experience. It became very clear to the group that although many of the skills are transferable, coaching is not just another name for mentoring. Coaching is very much about drawing out, whilst mentoring is more concerned with input.

Following this training, the group were asked to pair up and practise their newly acquired coaching skills on each other for the remainder of the summer term. We met again as a group twice during this period to 'catch up'. This was a very important part of the training, as it allowed those involved to consolidate their coaching skills, but also to highlight and discuss any issues, before 'going live'.

At a whole staff meeting at the end of June, the idea of peer-coaching as a service was introduced to the staff. Flyers were left in the staffroom, with a 'request for coaching' reply slip. The response to this was very encouraging ... and, it has to be said, quite surprising. Within a few weeks, enough 'coachees' had come forward, for most of the coaches to be paired up. When somebody came forward, asking to be coached I would set up an initial meeting with them. During this meeting, I would seek to clarify the issues and what they hoped to get out of the process, as well as discussing with them the best 'coaching' match for them. The issues they wanted to address were wide and varied. Some staff wanted to look at general issues such as behaviour management, whilst others wanted to look at very specific issues such as 'incorporating ICT into their lessons'. Following this meeting, I would discuss the issues with the coach who had been selected. If they were happy to proceed, I would then leave it up to them to arrange a time to meet the coachee and to get the process started.

When we were planning how the coaching sessions would work, we were all very clear about one thing – very little, if any, paperwork would be involved. The process was to be centred around professional dialogue and it was felt that writing out endless meeting notes, action plans and target sheets would not help the relationship between coach and coachee to grow.

The early signs from the coaching programme are very encouraging. The coachees are really appreciating being able to set their own agenda with a view to addressing their own issues, but with the support of one of their peers. The coaches are also commenting on how the coaching process requires them to be very reflective about their own practice – with very positive results.

It has been very interesting to see how, once you start to introduce coaching at a school, it begins to develop a life of its own. We now have many different strands of coaching developing at LCS. For example, some subject areas are setting up their own subject-related coaching programmes. Another example is senior leaders who have responsibility for a particular aspect of teaching and learning, e.g. ICT, Assessment for Learning and Literacy are putting together small groups of specialist coaches, to help colleagues develop these aspects of their teaching.

The next challenge with regards to coaching, as far as I am concerned, is to develop a 'culture of coaching' at the school. By this I mean moving to a situation where coaching is not an 'event' that happens to a small number of people, but instead it becomes the way in which the majority of staff at LCS interact, during their day-to-day work.

In 2004–5 we were fortunate enough to have a very strong group of NQTs completing their induction period at the school. As has already been mentioned, the support available to NQTs at LCS is very good. We have a strong team of mentors and a highly effective induction programme in place. It always seemed unfortunate that this structured support was not available to teachers in their second year of teaching – a time of consolidation, when structured support would still be beneficial to the developing teacher. This was one of the key reasons for setting up the Early Professional Development (EPD) programme. It was hoped that this programme would (a) introduce these staff to action research – a highly effective and worthwhile CPD activity – and (b) give them access to a coach, rather than a mentor, in their second year of teaching.

So what does the programme look like? At an NQT meeting in June 2005, the NQTs were asked to consider a particular aspect of their work, which they would like to carry out some action research on. It was important that this came from them and was not imposed on them. At the next meeting, a colleague from University College Chichester came to speak to the group about how to plan and carry out their action research. This helped to clarify a number of issues, such as: What do you want to find out? What evidence will you gather? How will you gather it? How will you analyse it? Following this, they were then asked to 'firm up' their proposals. A wide range of ideas were put forward:

Areas of focus
• Develop a linked Maths curriculum for pupils in the intervention programme and research current best practice for KS2 scores below L3
• Introduce an active policy for G&T pupils around the school for academic subjects. Involvement of school clubs, national competitions, etc.
• Raise achievement for EAL students in English at KS3/4
• Develop cross-curricular numeracy in Science
• Address the needs of Gifted and Talented pupils
• Consider the impact of single-sex classes in Science at KS4
• Examine Teaching and Learning styles at post-16 level in Physical Education
• Introduce individualized learning within the Business and Enterprise faculty

- Consider the impact of the national strategy on raising pupil achievement in KS3 English

- Explore the idea of an alternative curriculum and art therapy for disaffected pupils to boost confidence and self-worth

- Explore how subject specific key words can provide barriers to pupil progress

- Identify levels of achievement in mixed-ability classes and set classes and draw comparisons

- Coach disaffected pupils in KS4

On return to school in September, each member of staff who was to be involved in the EPD programme was allocated an EPD coach from the Leadership Group. The purpose of the EPD coach is to hold an initial meeting with the teacher, in order to plan their research project. This involves:

- clarifying the issues
- identifying what they really want to find
- planning how they will do it
- setting up an action plan – with timings.

Following this, each pair will meet regularly (once a half-term) to check progress, offer guidance/support, etc. This is yet another strand of coaching, which continues to evolve at LCS. The response to this has been very encouraging. Already one of the teachers who wants to look at supporting EAL pupils has arranged to spend a day at a school in Tower Hamlets, which exhibits best practice in this area.

The research that this EPD group carry out, will also inform one of their Performance Management objectives. This helps to support another target of the school, which is to raise the profile of Performance Management and link this to high-quality and effective CPD.

In the summer term 2006, all Year 2 teachers on the EPD programme will present their work and findings to the current cohort of NQTs during NQT meetings, with a view to sharing their good practice but also preparing the NQTs for the EPD programme.

Shaun Allison is Assistant Headteacher at Littlehampton Community School

For more information go to:

www.standards.dfes.gov.uk/research/   Follow the 'themes' link on the top left. This takes you to an index of different themes, for example, Assessment for Learning, Behaviour and so on. Select one of these. Then click the 'view all digests on this theme' link. This will then take you to an index of summaries of bits of research that have been carried out in this area. For example, in the 'Assessment for Learning' themes section, there is a piece that looks at 'How do pupils respond to assessment for learning'.

www.dfes.gov.uk/research/   This site provides details of all the research the DfES has commissioned or published since 1997. Key word searches can be carried out on certain topics.

www.gtce.org.uk/PolicyAndResearch/research/ROMtopics/   Here you will find a series of summaries of research on topics, which should be of direct interest to teachers. The format and content enables teachers to decide quickly if the research is interesting and relevant to them.

There is also some useful information on the CUREE website about the national framework for mentoring and coaching: www.curee-paccts.com/dynamic/curee48.jsp#Communicating.

Building capacity for further ongoing professional development

In this chapter the developmental nature of observations is considered with clear guidelines for carrying these out. Compare the observation practices of the author's school with your own workplace, and the way in which the Ofsted criteria for teaching and learning can be used to gain statistical evidence not only for school self-evaluation purposes, but also to evaluate the impact of ongoing professional development on classroom practice and student learning. The individual staff development pro forma provides a concrete overview of the needs of teachers following observation, which can be matched to modules from the DfES Pedagogy and Practice materials for the benefit of ongoing individual and team development and the students with whom they are working.

Classroom observation

The act of observing other colleagues or being observed in the classroom, has to be the singular most powerful way of improving our teaching and learning practices for the benefit of students. All too often, however, observations are carried out infrequently as a necessary, perfunctory requirement of performance review procedures. Add to this the reluctance of the observer to make challenging judgements against a set of observation criteria, for fear of damaging relationships with colleagues with whom he/she may have worked closely for years and it is not surprising that the tool of observation in our continuous professional development is frustratingly underused, to the detriment of generations of students.

What is necessary is to bring about a complete change of mindset in the way that we approach and view observations. We need to dispel fears, foster positive attitudes towards observations as a powerful developmental tool and somehow get away from the anxiety and disappointment we all feel when areas for development are identified in a lesson we had hoped would be viewed favourably against the most challenging of criteria. The importance of making accurate judgements is reinforced by the new-style Ofsted inspection which uses the accuracy of the school's self-evaluation procedures to guide and inform the external inspection team's 'trails' within the school. The quality of teaching and learning in the school is informed to a large extent by the judgements made through observation of lessons. It is crucial that the overall judgement in this area is an accurate one and based on rigorous evidence gleaned from embedded systems and procedures.

Most schools and colleges will have their own ways of carrying out observations. I am happy to share here what we do at my own school which may be of use if you wish to compare or re-evaluate the systems in place in your own context. So much has been written regarding appropriate procedures and protocols surrounding the observation process that it would be superfluous to do so again here. However, I feel that the following are key elements of basic good practice for anyone observing a colleague for either monitoring or developmental purposes, both of which usually apply:

✓ There should usually be some negotiation about which lesson is to be observed; this should be agreed well in advance. It may be necessary to request to see a specific lesson or group in order to observe specific teaching and learning skills.

✓ The observer should be provided with a comprehensive lesson plan such as the one outlined in Figure 5.1, with any additional resources or worksheets attached.

✓ A focus for the observation should be agreed in advance which can then provide the backbone of developmental feedback and self-reflection, although more general feedback will also usually be appropriate.

✓ If possible, time should be allowed to provide some informal feedback at the end of the lesson, although it is important that this should not contradict more formal, written feedback later. It is usually possible to pick out one or two features of the lesson which were positive and which will encourage the member of staff rather than demoralize them. Guard against leaving the person you have observed with only critical and negative comments, which may damage confidence and morale; areas for development or of serious weakness are best discussed face to face and with time for constructive ways forward to be considered.

✓ Adequate time should be set aside for formal feedback without interruptions as it is vital that colleagues feel valued and that due weight and importance is given to the process as a whole. If possible this should be timetabled into the observation procedures in advance and should occur within two to three days of the observation taking place. The concept of a dialogue around the observation is a good one to keep in mind and will afford productive outcomes for both participants. A way into the discussion may be to begin by asking how well the observee felt the lesson went.

✓ There may be times when it is necessary to be quite challenging with some of the judgements you are making. If this is the case, always bear in mind that the person you are observing is *entitled* to professional, honest and constructive feedback which will move him/her forward in their practice. Be confident that you are making a difference not just to a colleague, but to students' learning in classrooms.

✓ Remember that all staff are entitled to an observation process which is underpinned by the highest professional standards throughout; modelling this is good CPD in itself.

✓ Paired observation is excellent CPD to enhance the skills of observers. The follow-up discussion of a lesson observation carried out in this way is often fascinating and skill-enhancing. It will also improve the confidence of those who are called upon to make judgements about the performance of other colleagues while making the feedback for the observee still more focused, accurate and valuable.

✓ Wherever possible and with appropriate arrangements, support staff should be included in observation procedures, for example Learning Support Assistants and Cover Supervisors.

The pro forma in Figure 5.1 was designed by a colleague on the SLG at my school to support colleagues towards successful practices in the classroom and it is one that I encourage all staff to use not just when being observed, but at any time. The principles of successful teaching and learning are embedded in it, which means that from the outset key success criteria underpin the preparation and planning of a lesson. A good place to start!

At my school we have adapted the Ofsted criteria for teaching and learning into one pro forma (Figure 5.2), although this is constantly evolving and under review; you may see the criteria used in places as Inadequate, Satisfactory, Good and Outstanding. This process is supported by a clear guidance booklet for all staff which emphasizes our entitlement to a fair, challenging and consistent process of observation across the school.

This has obvious benefits:

1. Colleagues are prepared for the type of judgements made during an external inspection process.

2. By collating judgements made on individual teaching and learning practices across the school, we are in a very strong position to provide powerful evidence of the overall judgements in this area on the school SEF.

3. Collating and analysing the separate strands of criteria provides individuals with a clear idea of their strengths and areas for development in classroom practice. Any developmental needs can therefore be planned for by including them on the the individual staff development pro forma and improvements in practice identified in future observations should the judgement move up the scale. How encouraging for all of us to be able to measure improvements in our practice.

4. Statistical analysis of the overall observation grading of lessons for an individual, faculty and across the whole school can provide important evidence of the impact of CPD on both teaching and learning if tracked over time. What is more, a detailed analysis of individual strands of criteria within a faculty and across the school can be a powerful and accurate way of identifying specific strengths in teaching and learning as well as informing future planning for CPD to target areas for development. These can then be included in team or whole-school improvement planning.

5. Individuals or departments demonstrating excellence or expertise in a given aspect of teaching and learning can contribute to the development of other individuals or teams where practice is less strong. This is where the role of the CPD co-ordinator is invaluable in aiding the dissemination of good practice through facilitating collaborative projects, coaching partnerships and helping to establish networks for learning conversations as powerful CPD tools to impact on classroom practice and student learning.

6. Following on from point 5 above, co-ordinators will now be in a strong position to draw up an 'excellence directory', which will, hopefully, include a wide range of staff based on sound evidence gleaned from observations. This tool will then provide CPD co-ordinators with a fantastic pool of expertise which can be deployed as above or through establishing an effective cycle of peer observation.

Figure 5.1 Lesson preparation and planning pro forma

Teacher:		Date:			Subject:	
Day:					Period:	
Year group:		Students present:		NOR:		Ability:	H = High I = Intermediate L = Low M = Mixed

Topic:	Targeted attainment range (NC levels/GCSE grades):
SEN information (IEPs etc.):	LSA support in lesson – Name/Involvement:

Continuity with previous work:

Learning objectives for today:

Lesson content summary

Starter:

Main Activity(ies):

Plenary:

Differentiation:	Resources:
Consideration of Literacy/Numeracy/ICT/ Citizenship/Health & Safety:	Homework and date due in (if appropriate):

Content for next lesson – points/individuals to follow up:

Figure 5.2   Lesson observation pro forma

Anytown School

Observation Schedule

Teacher: .... Date: ....   Period: ....
Observer: ....   Pupil nos: ....
Topic: ....   Group: ....

Summary

General overview of lesson including general management of pupils, expectations and working environment.

Teaching

Evaluate the extent to which the teacher:	I	S	G	O
a. Shows expertise in the subject areas of learning, subjects and courses				
b. Plans clear learning objectives and suitable teaching strategies				
c. Interests, encourages and engages pupils – maintains a good pace through lessons				
d. Challenges pupils and expects the most from them – promoting equality of opportunity				
e. Uses methods and resources enabling all pupils to learn effectively – differentiation				
f. Insists on high standards of behaviour, using strategies to ensure effective use of time				
g. Makes effective use of teaching assistants and other support				
h. Uses homework to reinforce and extend what is learnt in school				
i. Uses assessment to improve planning and learning				

Learning

Evaluate the extent to which:	I	S	G	O
a. Pupils acquire new knowledge, skills, ideas and understanding				
b. Pupils are engaged, focused and work with application and care				
c. Pupils maintain a good pace of work and productiveness				
d. Pupils work independently and collaboratively				
e. Pupils of differing groups can progress				
f. Pupils' work is regularly assessed				
g. Feedback to pupils is constructive				
h. Students are involved in setting and reviewing targets				
i. Pupils understand how well they are doing and how they can improve				

Summary

Main strengths:

Areas for development:

Teacher comment

Overall grade:

Signed teacher: .... Signed observer: .... Date: ....

Figure 5.3   Quality of teaching and learning

Anytown School – Teaching

NAME: ....   DEPARTMENT: ....

Quality of teaching – evaluate the extent to which teachers:

a Show good command of areas of learning, subjects and courses

Teachers have incomplete understanding of subjects or courses. Teaching is inaccurate.	Teachers have a secure understanding of the subject curriculum. Teaching is accurate.	Teachers have a good subject knowledge, drawing on a range of relevant examples.	Teachers have an expert knowledge of the curriculum, drawing on a wide range of relevant examples with links to other areas.

b Plan effectively with clear learning objectives and suitable teaching strategies

Teachers plan a limited range of strategies. Plans lack detail or have poorly detailed objectives.	Teachers make work varied. Lesson aims are clear and described to pupils at the outset.	Teaching methods are imaginative and individual needs are well catered for with clear learning objectives.	Teachers plan activities matched sensitively to pupils' needs with detailed learning outcomes.

c Interest, encourage and engage pupils

Teaching is dull and fails to capture pupils' interest and enthusiasm.	Teaching is sound and the work set fills time appropriately.	Teaching is imaginative, pupils are engaged in a range of activities and there is a good pace to the lesson.	Teaching is stimulating and enthusiastic. Pupils are actively and enthusiastically engaged in a wide range of activities.

d Challenge pupils, expecting the most from them, promoting equality of opportunity

Teachers' sights are set too low and they accept pupils' efforts too readily with little recognition of individual need.	Tasks have sufficient challenge to keep pupils working. Successful provision for pupils who respond poorly to school or have difficulties in learning.	Teachers expect pupils to work hard, the level of challenge is realistic and all pupils are productive. Individual needs are well catered for.	Teachers expect pupils to work hard, the level of challenge is realistic and all pupils are productive. Individual needs are well catered for.

e Use methods and resources that enable all pupils to learn effectively

Activities planned are mundane with limited tuning to individuals' needs.	Teachers seek to involve pupils productively in lessons. Pupils are given scope to make choices.	Teachers understand the next steps needed in pupils' learning, providing a wide range of activities to help.	Teaching methods are well selected. Activities and demands are matched sensitively to pupils' needs.

f Make effective use of time and insist on high standards of behaviour

Inadequate	Satisfactory	Good	Outstanding
Greater effort is exerted on managing behaviour than learning. Groups of pupils cannot cope and misbehave.	Relationships are constructive and there is sensitivity to the needs of individuals and groups.	Teachers and assistants relate well to pupils with good, well managed interactions with pupils.	There are excellent relationships in the class. Pupils support each other and work at a very good pace.

g Make effective use of teaching assistants and other support

Inadequate	Satisfactory	Good	Outstanding
Teaching assistants provide an extra pair of hands but little effective support for learning.	Teaching assistants are adequately prepared to contribute to pupils' learning.	Teaching assistants are well deployed and make a significant contribution.	Well directed teaching assistants and paired or joint teaching reinforce and strongly support teaching.

h Use homework effectively to reinforce and extend what is learnt in school

Inadequate	Satisfactory	Good	Outstanding
Homework is rarely set or marked and is often a routine task that does not extend the work from lessons.	Homework extends class learning. Pupils are given scope to make choices and apply their own ideas.	Homework is well considered and assignments effectively extend what is learned in lessons.	Homework is challenging and planned carefully to interest pupils, and develop their skills and their subject understanding.

i Use assessment to improve planning and learning

Inadequate	Satisfactory	Good	Outstanding
Insufficient use is made of assessment in planning pupils' work and pupils have little idea of their own progress.	Teachers know pupils' recent progress and base their plans on this information. Pupils know how well they are doing.	In class questions are well targeted so that progress is checked. Pupils know how well they are doing and how to improve.	Progress checks are used to reshape teaching. Pupils are helped to judge their own work and to set targets for improvement.

 Photocopiable: The CPD Co-ordinator's Toolkit

NAME: ....   DEPARTMENT: ....

Quality of learning – evaluate the following:

a How well pupils acquire new knowledge, skills, ideas and understanding

Pupils can explain confidently and clearly what they have learnt, using a very good range of research tools including ICT.	Pupils work hard to interpret tasks, applying initiative well. They ask questions that show a desire to learn.	Pupils are concerned to progress with tasks, using some initiative in researching and presenting ideas.	Pupils make little effort to understand tasks set, with limited initiative and poor presentation of work.

b How well pupils show engagement, application and concentration in their work

Pupils show very good motivation, commitment and progress, applying intellectual and other skills well.	Pupils show good motivation, applying a range of skills in new contexts to carry out tasks.	Pupils' motivation, concentration and commitment is sound, with appropriate use of skills and understanding.	Motivation, concentration and commitment of pupils to tasks is low; they do not apply prior learning well.

c Pupils' pace of working and level of productiveness

Pupils plan the use of the time very well to meet fully the requirements of the task with work of high quality.	Pupils concentrate well, working hard to produce good quality work meeting the requirements of the task.	Pupils show sound concentration and pace of working, completing tasks to an appropriate standard.	Pupils' concentration is poor. Work is at a slow pace with tasks incomplete and poorly produced written work.

d How well pupils work independently and collaboratively

Pupils use time well, making the most of choices offered and showing very good initiative and independence.	Pupils show enthusiasm for the tasks they are set, selecting the appropriate resources for the task.	Pupils show sound interest in their work, sharing responsibility for completing collaborative tasks.	Pupils show little interest in lessons and are reluctant to use their initiative or to work independently.

e Progress of different groups in lessons (ability, gender, ethnic, EAL)

They are very well motivated making very good progress, with work showing originality and attention to detail.	They have positive attitudes, are actively involved and make good progress. Their work shows good attention to detail.	They show sound motivation and commitment to their tasks and are satisfied with their own progress.	Pupils' groups show low commitment to tasks and make unsatisfactory progress.

	Inadequate	Satisfactory	Good	Outstanding
f How thorough assessments of pupils' work are	Work is not marked or marked infrequently.	Work is marked regularly and recorded systematically to track progress.	Marking gives teachers a clear understanding of pupils' skills and understanding.	Pupils' work is assessed thoroughly. Oral interactions in class are well geared to check and develop understanding.
g How constructive assessments are	Marking does little to help pupils improve.	Teachers let pupils know how well they are doing.	Marking is diagnostic and helps pupils to improve their work.	Pupils receive well focused critiques of their work, helping them see how to improve.
h How well assessment is used to inform planning and target setting	Insufficient use is made of assessment in planning pupils' work. Targets set for most pupils are too low, too high or too general.	Teachers know what pupils have achieved recently and base their plans on this information. They use assessment information to set targets.	In class questions are well targeted so that progress is checked. Assessment information is used well to set challenging targets.	Progress checks are carefully designed and used to reshape teaching. Assessment information is shared between parents and staff.
i Pupils' understanding of how well they are doing and how they can improve	Pupils are given little idea of how well they are doing.	Pupils are aware of the overall quality of what they have done.	Pupils are regularly involved in helping to assess their own work.	Pupils are helped to judge their own work and to set targets for improvement.

 Photocopiable: The CPD Co-ordinator's Toolkit

The following case study provides powerful evidence of the developmental nature of observation, the principles of which can be applied to many contexts.

CASE STUDY

Modern Foreign Languages department use of developmental observation as CPD

Providing CPD opportunities for a large department/faculty within time and pecuniary restraints has provided a challenge which has led us as a school to reappraise our CPD strategies and practices. At the same time we have developed procedures for monitoring and evaluating the success of CPD activities. It is essential that each of us proactively engage in CPD activities be they external courses provided by the LEA (Local Education Authority) or other external providers, or school-based activities with a clear focus and measurable outcomes.

Each year following performance reviews with our line manager, we set ourselves three targets: one is linked to our examination results, the second and third directly to our professional development. The second and third targets are often set as a result of lesson observations. As a head of department it is my task to provide a planned programme of CPD activities which will help individuals to meet these agreed targets sometimes in line with whole-school objectives as identified on the SIP. I must also evaluate whether these targets have been met, as well as whether the CPD activities have been successful, particularly in terms of changing teacher behaviour, enhancing skills and knowledge, and impacting on students' learning.

The individual staff development pro forma is helpful in outlining a wide range of creative and diverse ways of providing effective CPD opportunities for individual teachers within this large department. A key factor in successful CPD provision is the use of classroom observations which provide an opportunity to set agreed targets. These could be any of the following:

- to improve use of the target language
- to ensure there is good pace in the lesson
- to set tasks of a more challenging nature
- to ensure clear learning objectives are outlined at the beginning of the lesson.

Once the reviews are completed and the targets are agreed, we use the individual staff development pro forma to help us to decide the most appropriate CPD activity which will enable individuals to meet their targets.

If, for example, a colleague's target is to improve his or her own use of target language in the classroom, he/she may request to observe some lessons where good practice already exists. In addition, it may be suggested that he/she does some research on the subject and prepares a presentation at a departmental meeting which then has the benefit of every teacher hearing new ideas on the use of target language in the classroom. As a follow-up the teacher in question will be observed again with a focus on use of the target language, enabling an assessment to be made not only based on to what extent the teacher has met his/her target, but also to evaluate the CPD activities put in place to help the teacher towards meeting it.

One of the benefits of working in a large department or faculty is the wide range of expertise available. As a result, peer observations have been one of the most useful developmental strategies available to us.

Mary joined us as an NQT. Observations carried out by me and the induction tutor highlighted the following strengths in her classroom practice: excellent use of target language, very good

---

classroom management, excellent subject knowledge and good planning which ensured coverage of the four skills of listening, reading, writing and speaking.

It was identified, however, that the majority of activities she planned were led by her and that pupils were not given many opportunities to work in pairs or groups. One of the agreed targets at her interim review was to provide activities which would encourage her pupils to work collaboratively. Through discussions with me, a programme of observations of capable practitioners was planned for her over a half-term period. At her fortnightly meeting with her mentor she discussed the activities she had seen and how she could incorporate them into her own lessons. At the end of the year Mary was observed by the LEA adviser for MFL who made a very positive comment about her group and pair work. Not only did this positive feedback boost Mary's confidence and provide indisputable evidence of her development in this aspect of her teaching, it also helped me to evaluate the effectiveness of the CPD provided.

With the arrival of interactive whiteboards in classrooms across the department, it was evident that many of us would need training to enable us to use them effectively. At the time over half the colleagues in the department had identified the need to extend their knowledge and use of interactive whiteboards as an important target, which linked to whole-school targets for improvement in the use and implementation of ICT across the curriculum. Through lesson observations it became clear which staff had the greatest level of expertise in this area. We had recently been joined by two highly enthusiastic teachers who had some knowledge and practice in the use of the interactive whiteboard, and who agreed to share their expertise and help provide training for the benefit of other colleagues. They were also keen to extend their own knowledge and skills, which working together to provide departmental Inset also allowed them to do. They were motivated in addition by having the opportunity to take forward a departmental initiative thus giving them both valuable leadership experience.

Their first planned activity was to teach two lessons to be observed by other colleagues in the department, during which they demonstrated various ways in which the interactive whiteboards could be used. Secondly, they used the departmental CPD Inset day to show colleagues how to put together a PowerPoint presentation and to give us all a topic linked to a specific year group which we worked on during the rest of the session applying our new skills. Not only did we gain valuable training in how to put a presentation together, we also finished the session with seven different PowerPoint presentations which were put in our departmental shared area for us all to use. Subsequent lesson observations clearly demonstrated that these CPD activities helped staff to achieve their target to use the whiteboards more in lessons. This also impacted on students' enjoyment of lessons as evident in student feedback.

As teachers we are often reluctant to share our ideas. One of the greatest benefits to my own teaching has been the accumulation of ideas gained from lesson observations. With this in mind we set up a series of peer observations in the department. As this was going to be the first occasion that some of us had been observed by another colleague within the department we decided that this was to be done on an informal basis. We agreed at our next meeting that we would report one activity which we felt had been particularly effective or innovative. At the end of the period of observations, in our meeting slot under the heading of CPD, we each shared one teaching strategy or game we had observed that was new to us which we agreed to incorporate into the planning of future lessons. Follow-up lesson observations demonstrated indisputably that across the department as a team we were deploying a far wider range of lesson activities to engage our students. Once again the feedback from students was very favourable.

Jayn Witt is Head of MFL, Millais School Horsham

Encouraging a 'Learning from each other in the classroom' approach

Observing good practice to improve teaching and learning skills has to be one of the most powerful tools in our professional development toolbox, yet once out of the induction year it would appear that many teachers have little access to the classrooms of other colleagues. This is a shame as the process of focused observation can have a notable and immediate impact on our practice. By now, as co-ordinator, you should have some secure systems for establishing the strengths and areas for development of individuals or teams in your school. In larger schools, your work will have enabled middle leaders to have clear systems for identifying and recording these with the objective of planning to support colleagues to develop their classroom practices. Staff should therefore be encouraged to carry out peer observations of skilled practitioners either in their own school or in local schools as a cost-effective, enjoyable and valuable way to increase their skills, knowledge and repertoire of effective classroom strategies. It is interesting to consider the range of teaching staff who would benefit from this kind of observation regardless of their experience, length of time in the profession or stage of their teaching career. These could include those teachers who are:

- ✓ NQTs or in their second or third year as part of their early professional development
- ✓ returning to the profession following a period of absence
- ✓ required to teach a new or second subject of which they have little or no experience
- ✓ facing a new challenge in the classroom, for example, working with pupils who have special educational needs
- ✓ about to change phase, key stage or year group
- ✓ unable to observe their own year being taught in their current school
- ✓ working in a support capacity
- ✓ aspiring to middle leadership
- ✓ looking to develop their observation skills
- ✓ keen to see new practice/ideas in action.

This type of peer observation should be underpinned by an agreed set of protocols which may look something like the following.

Arranging a good practice visit – guidelines for members of staff

- ✓ Plan your visit carefully. Have a clear and agreed focus for your observation and consider expected outcomes and impact on your classroom practice well in advance.
- ✓ Negotiate a date for your visit and clarify and agree how you will record the learning outcomes of your visit with the person you are observing, as a matter of professional courtesy.
- ✓ Build in sufficient time with the person you are observing to enable you to be involved in a learning conversation following the lesson.

✓ Plan time with your line manager in advance of the visit, to establish when you will discuss and evaluate any learning outcomes plus the future action you will take as a result.

✓ Ensure that you record the evidence, outcomes and action points in your professional portfolio.

Arranging a good practice visit – guidelines for middle leaders/line managers

✓ Support individual colleagues to agree an appropriate focus for the observation which will impact on his/her classroom practice. Ensure that correct professional protocols for the visit have been followed.

✓ Give due weight and importance to the follow-up discussion of learning outcomes with colleagues, no matter how busy you are.

✓ Consider how the outcomes of any observations can be disseminated or shared if appropriate.

✓ Guide colleagues to consider expected impact on classroom practice. Make plans to monitor and evaluate how successful and accurate observations have been in developing the member of staff and in having a positive impact on student learning in the classroom. If a series of observations supports a more formal professional target, you may wish the member of staff to complete an evaluation of the impact of planned CPD activities pro forma outlined in Chapter 6.

✓ Encourage and guide staff on how best to record evidence of developmental impact in a professional portfolio.

Using the DfES Pedagogy and Practice materials

I have to admit to being quite excited when I was first introduced to a box of materials produced by the DfES which provided much needed concrete support for teachers to develop a wide range of pedagogical and classroom skills. I have no doubt that there are countless ways to use them to support the professional development of staff working either individually, in pairs or in small working groups within a school, or 'buddying' with colleagues in other schools. However, if you have found the individual staff development pro forma, which was outlined in Chapter 2, useful and built the completion of it into part of your whole-school planning for CPD, you will find yourself in an excellent position to encourage focused use of the modules and may experience just a little glow of satisfaction as you do so!

It suddenly came to me that the information on the individual staff development pro forma completed by staff provided yet another opportunity to match a professional need with a focused CPD activity. I carried out an audit of each member of staff's area(s) for development as identified in that section of the pro forma and matched these with a relevant Pedagogy and Practice module which I felt would provide support. Each member of staff then received the memo shown in Figure 5.4.

Figure 5.4 Pedagogy and Practice memo

To: [Name of teaching staff]
Faculty/Department:
cc:
Date:

Continuing Professional Development 200X/Y

Following an analysis of your individual Continuing Professional Development pro forma, I see you have identified the following individual target(s) to support your ongoing development.

Target/skill area

- Starters and Plenaries
- Assessment for Learning

The school has recently obtained some interesting support material entitled 'Pedagogy and Practice' – a series of teaching modules designed to enable self-study. I list below the module(s) that most closely matches your needs and which may be of interest. You may wish to work through a module to support your ongoing development in this area; this may also be a good performance review target. Please discuss this further with your line manager.

Module 5

Starters and Plenaries

1. Starters and plenaries in the context of interactive teaching
2. What makes an effective starter?
3. What makes an effective plenary?

Module 12

Assessment for learning

1. What is assessment for learning?
2. Sharing learning objectives and learning outcomes
3. Helping pupils recognize the standards they are aiming for
4. Peer and self-assessment
5. Providing feedback
6. Reviewing and reflecting on assessment

Please note: these are just suggestions. I am happy to share the content of the module(s) with you to ensure it/they match your needs. For your information, there are accompanying video sequences on available DVDs to support and enhance the modules.

Best wishes

CPD co-ordinator

I then collated all this information and sorted it into departments/faculties/teams. Consequently, each head of department and the relevant senior line manager also received a résumé of staff observation needs matched to a relevant module, which they could use to support their leadership of CPD. With the recent workforce reform agenda impacting noticeably on the time available for teaching staff to focus on teaching and learning, this modular approach to staff development is a perfect developmental activity to engage and to develop our skills in the job we were trained to do.

'Positively reframing' observations

We should never underestimate the role we have to play as CPD co-ordinators in supporting the continuance of a positive mindset and culture of CPD practices in our workplaces. One brief conversation I had with a new member of staff illustrates this beautifully. Sarah (name changed) asked to see me regarding what she called a staff welfare issue. She appeared in my office at the agreed time and was visibly anxious and tearful. It transpired that this anxiety stemmed from the fact that she was due to be observed by her head of department within a couple of days. The chosen lesson was to be a Year 10 group which Sarah said she found to be quite challenging given that the behaviour of some students was disruptive. Individual students had failed to respond to some of the strategies she had tried and she felt she was not succeeding with the group as a whole. Sarah admitted that she was embarrassed about what she perceived to be a failing on her part to engage the group. She asked if I could speak to her head of department and request that she be allowed to change the observation to another time and with another group.

Sarah and I discussed the purpose of observations at length. I suggested that she 'reframe' the perception she had of this forthcoming observation and view it as an *opportunity* to request some advice and feedback from an experienced practitioner which would give her some constructive ways forward with behaviour management strategies. We talked about her *entitlement* to support from her line manager and how this could only impact positively on the teaching and learning in this particular classroom. Sarah agreed to speak straight away to the person who was to observe her. She left my office looking visibly relieved and said that had not really considered 'looking at it that way'. She was open with her head of department about the fact that she was finding the group challenging and asked if the focus of the observation could be on behaviour management.

Sarah came to see me after a few days and went through the whole observation procedure as she had found it. She was upbeat and admitted to being 'really pleased' with the outcomes. Not only had clear strengths been identified for her, of which she was very proud, she was already implementing some of the strategies suggested by the observer and was developing confidence given the positive effect that these were having on the group.

And *that* is what developmental observation is all about!

Points to remember

- Staff have an entitlement to a transparent, fair and consistent approach to observations which will support their ongoing development.
- Never be afraid to identify underperformance; this would not be supportive of individual staff development.
- Encourage peer observation within and outside your school context as cost-effective and valuable CPD.
- Support staff or team leaders of staff to meet ongoing development areas in creative, targeted and cost-effective ways.
- Challenge any negative mindset of staff towards observations and help them to see the beneficial outcomes for their CPD.

Further guidance on peer observation can be obtained by consulting The Teachers' Professional Learning Framework available from the GTC which can also be downloaded from www.gtce.org.uk/pdfs/peer.pdf.

The Ofsted site is a useful reference point. Download a copy of 'Good Teaching, Effective Departments' by going to www.ofsted.gov.uk/publications/index.cfm?fuseaction=pubs.summary&id=1245.

CHAPTER 6

Evaluating the impact of all CPD activities on both staff development and student progress: making a start

> Monitoring and evaluating the impact of CPD is often a neglected area of CPD systems and procedures in a school or institution. Using Thomas Guskey's five levels of impact evaluation, this chapter will support the work of CPD co-ordinators by examining one approach through which the key principles of good practice can be applied. Consideration is also given to the need for CPD co-ordinators to exploit the rapid technological advancements of the past few years in their future work.

Evaluating the impact of CPD

This aspect of our role has to be the one which gives CPD co-ordinators the most anxiety as we struggle to appreciate how to go about measuring impact and then how to use this information to feed back into the process of whole-school and individual planning for CPD. It is important that we recognize the complex nature of impact evaluation and that we appreciate that very few of us have really cracked it. Having said that, we are not complaining! There are exciting opportunities here for us to develop our practice in this area, to create innovative tools which will move our schools forward and to share these through viable networking communities in the true spirit of collaborative CPD approaches.

The recent research document entitled *Evaluating the Impact of Continuing Professional Development (CPD)* (available on the DfES website – see the end of this chapter) put together for the DfES by researchers from the universities of Newcastle and Warwick, provides a fascinating overview of the way that impact is measured across a range of schools. However, I intend here to put forward some practical ideas which will give you an immediate way into beginning to consider how we measure and monitor the impact of CPD across a school or institution, and the key elements of recognized good practice in this area; if we know what these are then we can develop our systems and practices fit for the context of our own schools, confident in the knowledge that we are making progress in the right direction.

Simple steps forward

Before any formalized CPD activity takes place, such as a coaching partnership, external training session, use of Inset time, workshop, conference or developmental meeting, and so on, it makes sense to engage the participants in the process of considering the following:

1. What targets or objectives the CPD activity is designed to meet.

2. What the expected impact of engaging in the CPD activity will be.

3. What the outcomes will be in terms of the impact on classroom skills/strategies/ knowledge and how this will impact on the learning of students.

4. How the above can be measured.

The consideration of impact should begin well in advance of any CPD activity taking place if the whole process of engaging in CPD is not merely to be an ad hoc process or a one-off training opportunity with little consideration given to how this might benefit individuals, students or the school.

Research has shown that all too often in many schools, the only consensus to evaluating impact comes in the form of a participant satisfaction questionnaire. While this can be valuable in gauging positive or negative attitudes to CPD, the latter obviously having an adverse effect on staff motivation and commitment to their ongoing development, there are far more diverse and exciting ways of evaluating impact. Make sure you consider the five different levels of impact evaluation as outlined by Thomas Guskey (2005) when considering how you might develop tools which will be effective in evaluating the impact of CPD rather than merely gauging what participants thought of it. Guskey's five levels at which impact can be evaluated are as follows:

✓ participant reaction

✓ participant learning

✓ organizational support and change

✓ participant use of new knowledge and skills

✓ pupil learning outcomes.

Start by considering the following statements in relation to impact evaluation in your own school or workplace. How does each statement relate to what is happening in your own context?

● Dissemination, that is, sharing/cascading, of the content of CPD activities is not the same as evaluating the impact of it. What distinctions, if any, are made in your school to avoid falling into this trap?

● Completing a participant satisfaction questionnaire following a CPD activity should not be seen as an end in itself. If this is the case in your school, what other evaluation tools are available/could be used/might be relevant to the CPD taking place in your workplace in order to evaluate impact across all the levels outlined by Guskey?

● How far are you, or the colleagues in your school, fully aware that the main purpose of CPD is not just about changing teacher behaviour but more fundamentally about impacting on students' learning in the classroom? What should your role as CPD co-ordinator be in changing mindsets?

- The evaluation of the impact of CPD activities is only relevant for teaching staff. Given that the above is a common misconception, how will you begin to challenge this way of thinking in your school? How can you begin to build in evaluation tools which will consider the impact of CPD on all learners in the school and how this relates to students' learning outcomes in classrooms?

You will also need to consider different approaches by which to measure and evaluate both formal and informal outcomes of CPD.

Formal outcomes

These can include:

✓ the analysis of statistical data to measure the impact of CPD on student achievement through internal and external assessments

✓ the analysis of staff and student feedback questionnaires to provide quantitative evidence of positive impact on development of learning, knowledge and skills

✓ statistical analysis of the observation criteria strands based on Ofsted criteria to judge teaching and learning in the classroom (see Chapter 5)

✓ the analysis of impact of CPD on staff retention and recruitment in the school/workplace

✓ the analysis of staff and student absence rates and how this can be related to a positive learning culture and CPD activities in the school

✓ formalized outcomes through performance review procedures where evidence of progress in a particular aspect of teacher performance or student progress can be provided.

More informal outcomes

These can include:

✓ an increased feeling of positive general well-being in the school; both staff and students feel valued and that their learning needs are catered for

✓ that staff can articulate the culture of CPD within the school, 'This is how we do it here', and are proactively engaged in their own development; there is a sense of ownership

✓ informal dialogue and feedback at performance management reviews; positive staff attitudes, varied and innovative approaches to CPD taking place at individual, team and whole-school levels

✓ that feedback from students is generally sought and valued. This can feed into the ongoing CPD of a colleague or department or be used to evaluate the outcomes of it.

Practical ways forward

We are all often far too busy with day-to-day issues to have the time to sit down and develop practical tools to ensure we are carrying out our roles as effectively as possible. I have included below a practical, ready-to-use (or adapt) pro forma which will take your impact evaluation practice forward if you need some inspiration in this area. As always this is only one model which may or may not suit your current context in its present form. That is fine. By adapting it to suit, you will be moving forward on the right tracks and any improved versions can be sent to me! So much of our work is a work in progress which is what makes our roles so enjoyable.

Before sharing these ideas with you, it is important to outline on what principles I have based them. These come from simply reading the research document mentioned above plus my own experience which I know is not an isolated one.

- ✓ Much impact evaluation carried out in schools involves teachers filling out question-naires based on how satisfied they were with the CPD in question rather than consider-ing the learning gained from it and how this in turn impacts on students in classrooms.

- ✓ In my experience teachers rarely see the value of completing such questionnaires; they feel it is a perfunctory task which little benefits their ongoing development, that is, it is a waste of their valuable time.

- ✓ Completing a questionnaire may not be the most meaningful or valuable way of considering the impact of CPD on teaching and learning in classrooms; other more imaginative methods may help to engage colleagues in the ongoing learning process rather than seeing the activity as a 'one off' with little or no value in the long term.

- ✓ Allowing staff to choose the most meaningful mode of evaluation for themselves, would help to engage them more in the longer-term outcomes of CPD and may be more allied to the nature of the CPD in which they participated.

- ✓ Guskey's five levels at which the impact of CPD can be determined are reflected here as part of the drive for meaningful evaluation.

- ✓ There is some scope for evaluation of other factors such as the impact of venue, cost-effectiveness and incidental learning which can be shared, as an integral part of par-ticipant reaction to the CPD and which will provide important feedback at this level to the co-ordinator.

- ✓ Good practice in impact evaluation considers potential impact *before* an activity takes place and is an integral part of the planning for it. The evaluation of the impact of a planned CPD activity pro forma (Figure 6.1) complements and works in tandem with the individual staff development pro forma to ensure that your practices reflect a 'joined-up thinking' approach.

- ✓ The method of evaluation completes the cycle of good practice CPD by monitoring outcomes with a focus on student learning and progress, informing future planning and dovetailing with performance review procedures in school.

- ✓ Ongoing evaluation of CPD over time, constructed to run alongside ongoing CPD activ-ities, is dovetailed carefully with the cycle of performance review and interim review meet-ings which are timetabled into this process; that is, these are not just a 'bolt on' extra.

- ✓ Scope for a formative evaluation based on the outcomes of CPD is provided.

Figure 6.1 Evaluation of the impact of planned CPD activities pro forma

Using the information from your individual staff development pro forma, please complete the following table for each planned, formalized CPD activity before you participate in it. You will refer to this after the activity has taken place in order to record additional comments and outcomes.

Planned CPD Activity: .... **Venue/Date/Time allocated:** ....

Please indicate the number of your Preferred Evaluation Choice in the appropriate column marked PEC using this key:
1. Learning questionnaire   2. Learning discussion with line manager   3. Reflective learning log   4. Formally evidenced pupil learning outcomes with narrative
5. Classroom observation and follow up discussion   6. Review of students' work   7. Student interview or attitude measures, e.g. questionnaire

Expected teacher outcomes What skills will you develop and how do you plan to use them? What gains in knowledge do you expect to make and how do you see this making a difference to your teaching/leadership? What do you expect to be able to do that you can't do now?	PEC	Expected student outcomes What will be the impact on students' progress/learning in the classroom? What are the likely timescales for this?	PEC	Measurement of student learning outcomes How will you measure the impact of CPD on students' learning and the progress they make as a result? How will this be evidenced	PEC
Proposed modifications to the above in the light of CPD experience					
Actual outcomes (if different)					
Self-review/impact evaluation and evidence trail					
Line manager's review of expected outcomes					

Agreed future CPD needs linked to outcomes: .... **Agreed cost effectiveness score:** ....

It is inevitable that you will need to spend time working alongside staff in order to implement this new approach. One of the best ways I have found when introducing new ideas is to ask staff who are most resistant to change/most vociferous in their lack of support for new systems and procedures to give feedback on how these new processes work and what could be done to improve them. One of the worst mistakes I made when starting out full of passion and new ideas was to take any negative comments as personal criticism. Use opportunities like this to engage staff who may not always appear to be on side; you will usually find them keen to help, supportive, flattered at being asked to be involved and keen to work with you. In the rare cases where the outcomes are not so positive, remain focused and confident in your leadership.

Make sure you are clear about the systems you are introducing in order to communicate your ideas clearly to staff. The key features of the pro forma in Figure 6.1 have already been outlined but, in addition, you will need to explain the following:

✓ Formal evaluation in this detailed way should only be applied to two or three planned CPD activities of a more formal nature, for example, attending a regular network group; planned external input from the LEA or other CPD provider; attending an external course, conference or series of workshops; planned peer or line manager observations with a particular focus; an action research project undertaken over a period of time; coaching or mentoring partnerships over time with an agreed pedagogical focus perhaps using the 'Pedagogy and Practice' materials issued by the DfES, and so on.

✓ For each planned CPD input, the member of staff should complete an evaluation pro forma. The form is designed to avoid repetition when considering impact before CPD, immediately afterwards, and again after a period of time, which are best practice ideas identified in the DfES research document mentioned at the beginning of this chapter.

✓ Similarly, the review process can be built into existing Performance Management procedures to avoid impact evaluation becoming a 'bolt on' extra.

✓ As always, encourage staff to keep their professional portfolios updated with this powerful evidence, not only of impact evaluation outcomes but also of a proactive approach to their ongoing professional development.

✓ The pro forma encourages choice in the ways that individual staff wish to evaluate the impact of a CPD activity while also considering the evidence bank which will underpin changes in practice and evaluate outcomes particularly on student progress.

✓ Given the varied ways in which CPD happens on an informal, day-to-day basis, it would be impossible to evaluate all the ongoing CPD that staff value or participate in.

✓ The whole process should be considered a work in progress; feedback from all staff should be welcomed to refine and improve it.

In addition to the above and while still wishing to keep completion of paperwork or online pro formas to a minimum, the reaction of participants to professional development activities should not be lost as this provides valuable feedback for us as co-ordinators too. I have included here one possible front sheet which could be completed and copied to the co-ordinator in the usual way (Figure 6.2). You will probably have something very similar in your own school or institution which you wish to continue using, although what I have tried to do is to include some other best practice principles as thrown up by the research mentioned above in order to broaden the 'participant reaction' level of feedback.

Figure 6.2 Evaluation following planned CPD activity

Please complete the following after each planned CPD activity. This will provide the CPD co-ordinator with important information by which your reaction can be evaluated. You may keep a copy for your future reference.

Name:

Date:

CPD activity:

What was the purpose of the CPD activity? What objectives did it support you to meet?

1. Please indicate how cost-effective you felt the CPD was using a number from 1 to 10; 10 being exceptional value for money:

   What are your reasons for this judgement? *You may wish to consider how far the CPD activity met its stated objectives, will be of use to you/the school, has stimulated you to change current practice, will impact on student learning outcomes, etc.*

2. How did the venue support/detract from expected learning outcomes?

3. Please tick below where you feel there were any incidental or unplanned outcomes from the CPD activity which you feel will benefit:

   Students?

   Your faculty/team?

   The school?

   Other stakeholders?

   If so, please outline these briefly below. *You may be asked to detail these more fully with your CPD co-ordinator/line manager.*

It is important that information from the form (Figure 6.2) is collated following whole-school CPD or where groups of individuals have participated. This collated feedback should then be communicated back to staff in some way, perhaps online through a shared site or the staff intranet for example, with further opportunities for staff to reflect on the outcomes of the day and possibly to participate in online discussions with staff within and outside the school.

What the pro formas do not provide for

The following also needs to be considered:

✓ How we evaluate informal learning which takes place on a day-to-day basis in the variety of ways which we have illustrated to staff and which we have encouraged them to value.

In order to aid staff to capture the 'nuggets' of learning which take place on a day-to-day or more informal basis you could consider introducing a simple online pro forma, as in Figure 6.3, which can be completed throughout the year. The more formalized planned CPD activities which have been chosen for detailed evaluation of impact can be copied and pasted from the pro forma in Figure 6.2, and any additional more incidental or informal learning recorded. In this way staff are building a powerful learning journal which can be referred to at any time. In addition, the journal can form the basis of professional learning conversations on a formal or informal basis in order to keep a learning dynamic. The key here is that individuals are completing this for their own benefit and are therefore far more likely to feel positive about doing so. In addition to this, most teaching staff are actually extremely passionate about improving their practice in the classroom and are far more likely to engage with something that helps them in this way. What we must all consider far more thoroughly are the measurable outcomes in terms of what our students learn as a result.

Route map/tool kit – examine your school's practice against Guskey's five levels of impact evaluation

The DfES research document I have referred to earlier in this chapter, *Evaluating the Impact of Continuing Professional Development (CPD)* contains a series of charts based on Guskey's levels of evaluation which allow schools to examine their own practice rating themselves as Emerging, Establishing or Enhancing against a series of criteria.

The researchers' original brief, as it explains in the document, had been to collect examples of good practice, templates, and so on in the course of their work. As these proved to be extremely scarce, this brief became more developmental. The outcomes of this whole process, the Route Map and the Moving On sections which accompany each chart, provide an excellent means by which schools can self-evaluate and review their work in this area – the Moving On sections are full of practical suggestions, ideas and references which, used diligently, could transform the way we monitor and evaluate impact in our workplaces (see DfES website for full details).

Figure 6.3   Ongoing CPD reflective log/learning journal

This log can be used to record any learning from either formal or informal CPD activities ongoing throughout the year. It should benefit you personally and can be used as an ongoing reference or as part of the evidence of your personal and professional development through the year.

Date	Activity	What I have learned	How I will apply this in the classroom/other area of my work, e.g. leadership of my team	How I expect this to impact on the learning of my students

Points to remember

- Use Guskey's five levels of impact evaluation to ensure that you are measuring the impact of CPD effectively with an emphasis on student learning outcomes in the classroom.
- Ensure that any systems you put in place to measure impact dovetail smoothly with existing performance management procedures in order that time be used cost-effectively.
- Communicate systems clearly to all staff, investing time in doing so.
- Be prepared to explain the rationale behind current approaches if challenged.
- Engage staff in the processes in place by consulting regularly and asking for constructive feedback to refine them.
- Use the Route Map self-evaluation tools to establish where your school is in terms of evaluating the impact of CPD practices.

The role of the CPD co-ordinator in the future

You may find the rapid technological advancements of the last few years and the bewildering range of online CPD opportunities both exciting and overwhelming. As CPD co-ordinators we are charged with ensuring that the future professional development of staff in our schools exploits this tremendous potential for cost-effective learning and that we are instrumental in moving our institutions towards becoming confident in the use of a variety of innovative e-tools. We need to ensure that the CPD opportunities we encourage and provide increasingly help staff to engage with the technology available. By doing so we can also model pedagogical approaches which will resonate with our expectations of students in classrooms and which will equip them adequately for the workplaces and lifestyles of the future.

The World Wide Web has moved a long way over the last few years. Cheaper costs, improved technology and new innovations have allowed it to develop from a purely static repository of information to a more interactive medium, facilitating real-time interactions between users. The following list is by no means exhaustive but should give some indication of the exciting options available. If, when we read them, the definitions below sound like a foreign language to us, then we have some serious catching up to do to ensure that we keep abreast of developments in online learning and use them innovatively to support the future CPD needs of staff. The range of options includes:

✓ static web pages – for articles, periodicals and so on

✓ blogs (short for weblogs) – essentially an online diary. Many people use these to share their experiences on a day-to-day, week-to-week basis. The majority of blogs used nowadays allow other users to pose questions/comments to the blogger

✓ forums/news groups – these are online discussion groups dedicated to a particular subject which allow participants with common interests to pose questions and give advice

✓ videoconferencing – although this has been around for some time, many people believe that videoconferencing will become far more mainstream over the next few years as the costs for implementing this continue to fall

✓ Wikipedia – this is a free content, multilingual encyclopaedia written collaboratively by contributors around the world

✓ instant messaging – this is where participants are involved in an online conversation, file sharing, bulletin boards and videoconferencing

✓ Point to Point (PTP) software – this allows users to connect computers to each other directly over the Internet. In this way files can be shared without the need to have experience of writing web pages.

Innovative use of the above technologies has also led to the introduction of new learning tools for organizations. These include:

✓ webinar – short for web-based seminar, this is a presentation, lecture, workshop or seminar that is transmitted over the web; a key feature of a webinar is its interactive elements

✓ distance learning – this is a type of education, typically college-level at present, where students work on their own at home or at the office and communicate with faculty and other students via e-mail, videoconferencing, chat rooms, bulletin boards, instant messaging and other forms of computer-based communication; it also includes virtual learning environments, learning gateways and Internet portals

✓ multipoint videoconferencing – this allows three or more participants to sit in a virtual conference room and communicate as if they were sitting right next to each other.

The above list is not exhaustive and, by the time you read it, will probably fall short of illustrating the enormous number of e-learning facilities which we can exploit and which will allow us to extend our collaborative, sharing ethos to engage the expertise, knowledge and experiences of educational professionals across the entire globe!

The Teacher Training Resource Bank (TTRB) is a useful site and has an interesting article on student feedback for CPD. Find it at www.ttrb.ac.uk/.

Go straight to Teachernet at *www.teachernet.gov.uk/wholeschool/london/teachersandleaders/professionaldevelopment/londonslearning/principles/principle7/evaluation/* for more information on evaluation of the impact of CPD.

Evaluating the impact of Continuing Professional Development (CDP) Research Report No 659, can be found on the DfES website. Go to www.dfes.gov.uk/research. Choose DfES Research Website option. Search for Evaluating the Impact of CPD and choose the research information option.

References

Bubb, S. (2005) *Helping Teachers Develop*. London: TES/Paul Chapman Publishing.

Department for Education and Skills (DfES) (2001) *Teachers' Standards Framework*, September 2001. DfES 0647.

Department for Education and Skills (DfES) (2005) *Leading and Co-ordinating CPD in Secondary Schools*. Guidance Document. DfES 0188-2005G.

Earley, P. and Bubb, S. (2004) *Leading and Managing Continuing Professional Development*. London: Paul Chapman Publishing.

Guskey, T. (2000) *Evaluating Professional Development*. Thousand Oaks, CA: Corwin Press.

MacGilchrist, B., Myers, K. and Reed, J. (1997) *The Intelligent School*. London: Paul Chapman Publishing.

Twigg, S. (2005) Foreword to *Building the School Team*. London: School Workforce and Development Board.

INDEX